The Big House in a Small Town

The Big House in a Small Town

Prisons, Communities, and Economics in Rural America

Eric J. Williams

 PRAEGER

AN IMPRINT OF ABC-CLIO, LLC
Santa Barbara, California • Denver, Colorado • Oxford, England

Library of Congress Cataloging-in-Publication Data
Williams, Eric J.
The big house in a small town : prisons, communities, and economics in rural America / Eric J. Williams.
    p. cm.
Includes bibliographical references and index.
ISBN 978-0-313-38365-6 (hbk. : alk. paper)—ISBN 978-0-313-38366-3 (ebook) 1. Prisons—United States. 2. Corrections—Social aspects—United States. 3. Corrections—Economic aspects—United States. 4. Rural development—United States. 5. Community development—United States. I. Title.
    HV9466.W55   2011
    365'.973—dc22   2010045114

ISBN: 978-0-313-38365-6
EISBN: 978-0-313-38366-3

15   14   13   12   11   1   2   3   4   5

This book is also available on the World Wide Web as an e-book.
Visit www.abc-clio.com for details.

Praeger
An Imprint of ABC-CLIO, LLC

ABC-CLIO, LLC
130 Cremona Drive, P.O. Box 1911
Santa Barbara, California 93116-1911

This book is printed on acid-free paper ∞

Manufactured in the United States of America

For my Mother
For her many sleepless nights and for teaching me
that what might seem impossible was possible.

Contents

Preface

When I was in high school, a friend of mine was sentenced to several years in the Maine State Prison in Thomaston. I had gone to visit him a couple of times in the county jail while he was awaiting trial, my first visit to a jail. I distinctly remember wondering how a person could live day to day under those kinds of conditions. I later went to visit the man in the state prison. What I remember most was not the prison itself, but the town of Thomaston. Here was this idyllic coastal Maine town with towering pines and white colonial homes—something right out of a postcard. And yet what dominated the downtown was this huge, high wall that separated Maine's only (at the time) maximum-security prison from the tourist-perfect postcard. The prison was built in 1824, just four years after Maine became a state, and it was operational until 2002. It was the disconnect between town and prison that I remember most, not what the visiting room was like or anything that was said between my friend and me that day.

My interest in prisons continued through graduate school, and this project was born out of that interest. I had thought that I would write my doctoral book on the new wave of supermax prisons that were being built across the country. But as I delved into the subject, what ended up being most striking to me was where and how these prisons were being built. Thomaston was eager to rid itself of the giant wall and prison the town housed in its midst. Meanwhile, in nearby Warren, Maine, the state built its replacement, a maximum-security and supermax facility, although the state rents out space in the supermax prison to other states (Maine has the lowest incarceration rate in the country).

In reading about towns like Tamms, Illinois; Corcoran, California; and Florence, Colorado, one cannot help but be taken aback by the eagerness of these towns to land a prison facility. I read story after story of communities offering all manner of "goodies" to the government to convince the state or federal government to give them the precious jobs that would hopefully keep them afloat in a world economy that had passed them by. I wondered what would make a community so desperate that it would go to these lengths.

So I bought a travel trailer and hit the road. The result of my nearly two years of living in that trailer is the book you are now reading. I lived in an RV park on the border between Cañon City and Florence, across the street from the Wal-Mart and a trailer park overlooking Highway 180 in Beeville. As much as I could, I tried to immerse myself in the world I had chosen to study. Over and over, I heard residents' mixed emotions about the bargain they had made. "You hate to base your economy on a prison," was a sentiment that was much expressed during my time on the road. But that was the bargain they had made and now they had to live with that decision. It was through the eyes of the residents of Florence and Beeville that this project took shape. It would have been easier and less time-consuming to sit back and do an economic impact study, but it seemed to me that their voices were being ignored.

Also ignored, from my research, were the voices of prison administrators. They are the ones who move their lives and their families to these rural communities for the sake of their careers. But in these rural communities, they cannot just blend in and are instantly thrust into a role as community leader, something their training in the corrections field does not normally cover. This book attempts to explain their plight, as much as the town in which they are located.

It seems obvious to say that no book is the work of only one person. First and foremost, I want to thank my dissertation advisor, Milton Heumann, for his reading and rereading of my chapters and his constant feedback and support. The other members of my dissertation committee—Lisa Miller, Daniel Tichenor, and Wild Bill Haltom—also generously gave of their time and insights. W. Carey McWilliams gave great inspiration early on in the project and I was saddened that he passed on before the project was finished. I also want to thank the Evangelites family, who gave me financial support as well as the University and Bevier fellowship foundation. I would also like to thank my colleagues at Sonoma State and Dean Elaine Leeder, who has supported this project from the day I walked in the door. I also wish to thank my faithful research assistant Amanda Clarke, who managed to somehow pick through my vast mistakes and cleaned up my work immensely. Also to my students in CCJS 450, whom I tortured with several rough chapters and who gently gave me feedback that helped this project along.

There are too many people in Beeville and Florence to thank, but the people there opened their lives to me and helped in any way they could. I do feel that I need to specifically thank the employees in the Cañon City Local History Center and Marjorie Villani at Pueblo Community College. Without them, I never would have begun to understand Fremont County and its quirks. In Beeville, Doug Dretke, formerly of the Texas Department of Criminal Justice (TDCJ) and now the director of the Correctional Management Institute of Texas, has done more for me than I could ever express. Additionally, the TDCJ and Federal Bureau of Prisons opened their gates to me, as much as they could, and helped this project become much fuller and broader.

Finally, I must thank my family, specifically my mother, Priscilla Williams and my brothers, Danny and Kenny, as well as my girlfriend Emily Barouch, who listened to my constant complaining and feeble explanations as to why this project took so long. I would be remiss if I did not also thank two of my cousins. Paul Emple, who forgave me when I forgot to ask about his golf game and helped get this project off the ground, and Peg Emple, without whose support I never would have made it through graduate school. To my grandfather Philip, who never missed an opportunity to remind me of his friend who went from undergrad to PhD in, I think, about six weeks. I only wish you had lived long enough to see this project completed (and, more importantly, to see the Red Sox win another World Series). And to my dad, who also passed away few years ago, I miss you and know you would have been my one family member who would have read this entire book.

Chapter One

Introduction

Imagine that you are a state representative in Texas. You look out of your office window and see a large contingent of people holding a pep rally on the steps of the statehouse. One of the pieces of legislation under consideration on this day is an appropriations bill for the building of several new maximum-security prisons. A consent decree meant to end the longest prison reform lawsuit in American history required the state to build several prisons as soon as possible to ease overcrowding.[1] The assembled group has come from three hours away in several yellow school buses. They are holding large placards that say "Bee for the Max" and "We Want a Prison." There is a woman in a bee outfit dancing in the middle of the chaos. All of this effort is meant to garner your vote in hopes of having a maximum-security prison call their town home.

Or perhaps you are on vacation in Colorado. You are on you way to visit the Royal Gorge Bridge just outside of Florence. The bridge is the world's highest suspension bridge over a breathtaking box canyon with sheer walls over 1,000 feet high on either side. In classic American fashion, a developer has "improved" the canyon and bridge by adding a theme park, with an incline railway and "skycoaster" overshadowing the natural beauty of the place. As you flip through the radio stations, you come upon a local station holding a telethon. Interested in what charities the locals find important, you tune in for a while. You hear an impassioned speech by the mayor, but much to your surprise, it is not some deadly disease he is ranting about. Instead, he is extolling the virtues of using a federal prison as an economic development strategy. The point of this telethon is to raise $100,000 to purchase a piece of land that will be donated to the federal government for the prison complex.

Stories like this have become commonplace in rural America. Whereas the California Department of Corrections used to refer to the process of selecting a community to house a new prison as "DAD," or "decide, announce, and defend," today's process would better be described as "LLC," or "lobby, lobby, and celebrate." Communities vying for a prison now take part in a process in which the burden is no longer as much on the government to convince them of the benefits of having a prison, but on the town to show the government why they are the best location for the prison. Florence, Colorado, and Beeville, Texas, took part in this "prison derby" and, for better and worse, were two of the winners.

Considered foremost on the list of NIMBYs ("not in my backyard") or LULUs ("local unwanted land use") just 20 years ago, towns are now fighting to have states, private corporations, and the federal government put new correctional institutions in their communities. Where as little as 20 years ago the California state government was still working under its DAD vision of prison siting, some towns have ceased looking at prisons as NIMBYs and are lobbying hard to land one. In doing so, towns are giving all sorts of incentives to federal and state officials to locate prisons in their community.

Communities have given land, upgraded utilities, and all but begged the government to give them a facility. A town in Missouri wrote a song that they sang to the siting committee during their hearings. After the end of the oil boom left their economy in shambles, Hinton, Oklahoma, actually borrowed $19 million from American Express to build a prison and then hired a private prison firm to run it. In Tamms, Illinois, the staunchly Democratic town has a billboard thanking the Republican governor for putting the state's newest supermax prison there. In Stone Gap, Virginia, the town paid the local community college to start a guard-training program and sent 500 people to Richmond for the hearings on the siting to help them land one of the state's two new supermaxes. They landed both.

Places as disparate as Youngstown, Ohio, a former steel town, and Warren, Maine, a former fishing and timber stronghold, have turned to prisons as the solution to their economic woes. We are fast approaching the point at which 1 percent of our population is in prison[2] and the number of people incarcerated has more than quadrupled since 1980, leaving the state and the federal governments desperate for more prison beds.[3] A recent study by the Urban Institute found that in the last quarter of the 20th century, "[t]he rise in the number of prisons has been extraordinary . . . state prison systems grew from 592 prisons to 1,023 prisons."[4] Many of these prisons have been built in communities that historically have not had them. The Urban Institute's study of 10 states found that the number of counties with at least one prison had increased from 13 percent of counties in 1979 to 31 percent of counties in 2000.[5] Calvin Beale, a demographer at the U.S. Department of Agriculture, found that there were nearly 350 prisons sited in rural areas between 1980 and 2000 and that 60 percent of new prison construction between 1992 and 1994 occurred in nonmetropolitan areas.[6] The spread of prisons and the booming prison population make what was once a highly localized issue more national in character.

In her 2005 James Madison Award Lecture, Elinor Ostrum discussed this lack of interest in local issues by academics. In discussing criticisms of the Workshop in Political Theory and Policy Analysis, she states, "Colleagues in political science have frequently chided us for the many studies we have conducted on 'dull, unimportant local problems.'"[7] It is exactly one of these misnamed "dull, unimportant local problems"—the impact of a prison on a local community and the ensuing relationship that develops—that is at the heart of this book. I say "misnamed" because these are issues that are not "dull" and certainly not "unimportant."

Issues of local politics may not be as "sexy" as those that take place on the national level, but their effects are no less important to our larger community. Beyond the aforementioned prison-building boom and the spread of prisons throughout the country, this issue shows us much about rural America's struggle to survive in a changing economic world. Rural sociologists have long studied the trend of capital moving out of rural areas to urban ones. This drain has forced rural communities to be more proactive and innovative to survive. Prison building has become one such innovation.

This book is about the nuts and bolts of local politics. Studies of politics and prisons at the higher levels of government abound, but very little has been done to understand these entities on the micro level.[8] To just discuss the prison-building boom writ large is to forget that these prisons are actually built in towns. Although some large cities may be able to absorb a large facility with very little impact on the community as a whole, this is not the case in a small rural community, where the prison population may equal the population of free citizens.[9]

This chapter outlines the overall project of this book and gives an overview of the chapters to come. It gives some background on the two towns in my study, Beeville, Texas, and Florence, Colorado, and explains my broader interests in the study. I outline my framework for gathering information and give the basics of the models that I developed to discuss the relationship between the prison and the community.

Although the phenomenon of the big house in a small town is not a new one, the way prisons are sited certainly is. Corrections departments nationwide have seen a large shift in communities' reactions to the notion of having a prison in their town. Not only are there more prison towns, there are more towns clamoring to become prison towns. In one of my interviews, the former Director of Institutions for the Texas Department of Criminal Justice (TDCJ) discussed the last time the TDCJ had to fight to locate a prison in a community the way old-time baseball players discuss life before the designated-hitter rule was implemented. It is a bygone era, seemingly never to return. Towns are so eager to have a facility located in their community that Departments of Corrections no longer need to even consider communities that will put up a fight.[10] As Jimmy Turner, Vice President of Operations for Corrections Corporation of America, said with regard to prison siting, "[W]e don't have to sell it to a community. The community is knocking on our door. It used to be 'not in my back yard.' Now, they want it in the front yard."[11]

This book is a study of two of these new prison towns: Beeville, Texas, and Florence, Colorado. Both are small rural communities that began the lobbying process in the late 1980s. Beeville had fallen on hard economic times with the decline of the Texas oil boom, and Florence, although never an economic hot spot, lost a significant number of jobs and residents with the decline of the mining industry. Both communities worked hard to land a facility, Beeville from the Texas Department of Corrections (now TDCJ) and Florence from the Federal Bureau of Prisons (BOP), and both have since become the site of multiple facilities.[12] They are both examples of the new rural prison towns that have cropped up all over the country over the past 25 years.

Beeville is on the Gulf Coast of Texas, approximately 60 miles north of Corpus Christi and 90 miles south of San Antonio. It is in the heart of South Texas, but is over 30 miles from the nearest interstate highway. As of 2000, Beeville proper had 13,000 residents and Bee County had 32,000 residents. Florence, Colorado, sits where the Colorado Plains meet the Rocky Mountains, 30 miles west of Pueblo and 45 miles southwest of Colorado Springs. Like Beeville, it is 30 miles from the nearest interstate highway, but unlike Beeville, it is not the center of life in its county, Fremont; next door, Cañon City holds that honor.[13] Florence proper has just under 4,000 residents in a county of 46,000. Beyond the difference in size and location, there is one major difference between these two towns: Beeville's prisons are all state-run, whereas Florence lobbied the federal government for its facilities. This difference has large repercussions for the communities themselves.

RESEARCH QUESTIONS

I met Benny Johnson, former mayor of Cañon City and former official with the Colorado Department of Corrections (DOC) about a month into my stay in Florence. Originally, I set out to do a straight impact study of four towns and wanted to talk to Johnson because he was involved with the siting process from both the prison's and the local government's perspectives. This interview, in retrospect, shifted the focus of this study and showed the importance of on-the-ground research. Mayor Johnson is an affable but also volatile man (he once had to be restrained during a City Council meeting) and spent his career with the Colorado prison system and his retirement in local politics. His father had also worked for the DOC.

Johnson regaled me for two hours with stories of the old days of the DOC (his father brought inmates home to work around the house), the problems with opening a maximum-security prison before the fence was built ("we spent that first year chasing convicts all around the county"), and the problems of domestic violence with corrections workers. When I asked about Florence's choice to lobby for the prisons, despite research that the effects were minimal, Johnson said "you can't tell me that [Florence] wouldn't be a ghost town had they not gotten a prison."

After I managed to work out the triple negative in my head, I understood the logic of his comment. No academic study can predict the future. Florence's choice was made out of fear and desperation. The town had been stagnant or shrinking for many years, with few opportunities to offer its children and little reason for them to stay in town. The choice to lobby for the prison made sense at the time. And although few people outside of Florence might care if it ceased to exist, the people of Florence care. The choice to get prisons might not be rational from a purely economic standpoint, but from a social standpoint, it made sense.

City managers and local politicians were not reading academic journals to decide whether or not to respond to the Request for Proposals (RFPs) sent out by various governments for prison siting. They saw the potential for jobs and wanted to land those jobs for their towns. What I realized while I was on the road was that the economic data were somewhat superfluous to the discussion. I could not tell the city manager of Florence that they would not be a ghost town had they not gotten a prison. What I could tell the city manager of Florence or Beeville or of any rural community thinking about joining the growing number of rural prison towns was what they could expect once the prison opened. I could find out how the face of their community would change and what factors could lessen the potential negative impact. Rather than studying the economic factors, I would look at social and institutional factors and garner a better understanding of prison-community relations.

This book seeks to answer two questions. First, what has been the effect of the prison on the local government, including law enforcement and the courts? These towns have lobbied for prisons to save them from an uncertain economic future and in return, the prisons have promised to give them a stable employment base on which to build. So the question is whether or not the prisons have delivered on their promise and what the unintended consequences, if any, have been. Economic data and crime rates are useful, but they only take one so far. We also need to understand the effect as perceived by the citizens of the community to get the full picture.

Several scholars have argued that more rigorous quantitative work is needed to understand the impact of prisons on a town. For example, McShane, Williams, and Wagoner have argued that in a perfect world, we would be able to do survey data with a large random sample of people over several different periods of time over several different towns and find out if feelings about the prison change over time.[14] Although this is a justifiable and plausible argument, it is also the case that survey data are just one way of trying to answer this question. I argue much can be discovered by a more intensive data-collection method—immersion into the community. This type of research, whether called interpretive social science or participant observation, sets out to explain a specific culture from the insider's viewpoint. Rather than attempting to understand from afar, the researcher becomes a part of the culture to better comprehend its intricacies. Going beyond classic qualitative interview methods, I chose to live in each town for a period of time to try to find out what life was like from the ground up. Politicians and local elites will often have a very different outlook on things than that of the rest of the citizenry, and although much can be learned from formal interviews and traditional qualitative observation, there is a different reality that is more fully understood through participant observation.

For example, one of the major impacts that residents continually point to has been the change in the fabric of the community in one form or another, but there is no real understanding of what that (or terms like it) means. What was it that existed in the town before that has changed now? Is it an effect of the new people coming to the community who work for the prison, or simply having prisoners in their midst? Is there a racial component to this claim? The survey research seems to indicate that there has been a change in perception in the prison towns, but it is an issue that needs much further study.[15] This study seeks to shed some light on what sorts of assumptions are inherent in the making of this claim of community.

Myth making runs deep in these communities, not only when it comes to their community, but also when it comes to the effect the prison has had on their towns economically and socially. Despite the growing evidence that prisons have little effect on the economics of the community[16] and even more evidence that local governments have little control over their own economy no matter what they do, communities are still clamoring for a facility.

I also look at the nature of the relationship between local governmental and social institutions and the new prison in their midst. There are examples of former prison officials becoming local politicians after retiring and local politicians becoming lobbyists for the prisons after their terms were completed. Current prison employees have become city counselors and county commissioners as well as becoming involved in the local community in various other capacities. There is a relationship here, but it is one that we know little about. A prison is a seemingly autonomous institution—one that is run within its fences or from the state capital. This is not always the case because the prison has needs that must be dealt with locally.

Some issues that are raised might seem trivial to larger urban areas, but to a small town, any drain on its resources can be problematic. Prisons do not pay property taxes and they do not pay utility bills in the way that regular citizens do.[17] Most prisons pay a predetermined amount for water and sewer on the basis of capacity, not on an actual daily census.[18] Although the prison pays a fair price, they do not pay for improvements because money for upgrades comes from local property taxes or bond issues. Often prisons will allow their minimum-security inmates to do public works or community improvement programs, one way of attempting to pay the town without really paying.

From the prison's standpoint, it needs help dealing with issues such as escapes or drug muling, in which visitors and corrections officers smuggle drugs into a facility. The local police force often aids investigations into crimes committed inside of the institution. This is a drain on a community's very limited cash coffers. In one town, commuting prison employees claimed that they were profiled and given traffic citations on the way to and from work. Problems such as these must be dealt with locally, and the prison and the government need to find avenues through which to do so. This research investigates these avenues.

There have been few attempts to view prisons as a purely local issue. Prisons are not normally viewed, by academics at least, as local legal institutions that affect the local community and become important players in the local political scene. The end result of this is that in most ways, prisons never become more than some amorphous "thing" outside of a study of a local community or some pawn of broader policy decisions. We have lost the idea put forth by James Jacobs's work that prisons themselves matter in a political context.[19]

Additionally, the current studies only ask questions from the community's side of this relationship. This strategy assumes that the community alone has a role to play in the relationship that develops between town and prison, but that prisons do not. Once a prison opens, it becomes intertwined with the community and the relationship that develops is a reciprocal one. The prison can make some of the positive effects on a town more profound or even soften the blow of the bad ones. For example, the former head of investigations for the McConnell Unit in Beeville explained that if he prosecuted every crime committed inside of his facility, it would completely overwhelm the local court system.

This is one of the primary ways that this book differs from other studies of prison communities. Although several studies do a good job of looking at this phenomenon from the standpoint of the town, none look at what has happened from the standpoint of the local prisons.[20] They are a major part of this story but are ignored by scholars except as a non-descript entity or a policy choice. These studies assume that the prisons are almost interchangeable, even if they recognize different states, differing prison policies, or that there is some minor difference between prisons of a certain security level.[21] The best prison scholars understand that prisons are highly individualized and can differ greatly even within a larger prison system.[22] This is no less true in their relationship to a local community, and ending a study at the prison's walls tells only part of the story.

A second major difference is in focus. This book explores a local issue that is national in scope. I do not intend to draw this discussion into other debates, especially that of the prison-industrial complex. This study has implications for many other communities that have prisons or are considering getting them, but this is not a book about state or national crime policy. Although there are some strong studies available that do so,[23] this study is about the local tapestry of a prison town, an issue that has growing national implications given our ever-expanding prison population.[24] The TDCJ alone has facilities in 65 different Texas communities spread throughout the state, and the Federal BOP houses facilities in 92 towns across the country.

The third major difference between this and other works on this topic is methodological. At its core, this is a work of participant observation and an exploratory study aimed at hypothesis generation. The focus of my findings is based on interview data, but many of the questions asked in those interviews were drawn from local knowledge gleaned during my time living in each community. There are obvious questions to ask about the effects of a prison on a community, but there is a certain amount of "local knowledge" that one gains from immersing oneself in the life of a town.[25] For example, the issue of domestic violence by corrections officers was first brought up to me by a local resident in the course of a conversation at the local library, as was the notion that there might be some inherent difference between federal and state prison employees. These issues were then investigated in a more complete manner, but never would have been considered as important had I not been utilizing the participant method.[26]

BIG PICTURE

This research bridges two currently distinct literatures in sociolegal studies and criminal justice work. The first, which will be discussed more fully in the following chapter, is the legal ethnographic work that looks at communities and their relationship with the law and the legal system. Like the legal ethnographies, this research also uses an immersion method to understand community and their relationship to the law, but instead I look at a particular legal institution—the prison.

The second set of studies looks at prisons using a participatory method, but without looking at the institutional relationships with the outside world. I argue that the rise in prison populations and large-scale expenditures for new prison building has made prisons a much larger political issue and, by proxy, a much more political entity. Corrections nationwide now cost more than $65 billion.[27] They are not a small part of any government's annual budget because spending on prisons has increased nearly 150 percent since 1986 and 40 states now contract with a private entity for the management of some part of their prison system.[28] Budget crunches in several states have led to questions about alternatives to incarceration to save money.[29] At some point in the past, prisons may have been autonomous institutions that could be studied as such, but they are now a political entity as much as any other part of the legal world. Although some studies have begun to look at prisons in this way,[30] these studies only look at prisons as a state or national governmental political institution. This study does so and argues that, no different than courts or the police, prisons should also be viewed as a local political institution.

POLITICAL SCIENCE, CRIMINAL JUSTICE, AND PRISONS

In the 1970s, some political scientists began to see the importance of studying local criminal justice institutions as political institutions. Unfortunately, prisons were not included in that concentration. However, there was some interest in the intersection between local politics and institutions such as the police and trial courts. In their edited volume, James Klonoski and Robert Mendelsohn claim that "added attention has thus been given to the importance of the dominant values and institutions—including the legal system—of the local community as critical variables affecting the realization of equal justice."[31] This added attention seems to have been short-lived because little has been done since then linking these two institutions, at least in a political science context.

James Q. Wilson argued that more needed to be done to link the local criminal justice system and local politics and did so with his work on the police and their relation to local politics.[32] Kenneth Dolbeare makes a similar argument in *Trial Courts in Urban Politics* and in doing so links state trial courts and the local government to understand the impact they have on each other.[33] These works and those of others tried to argue that legal scholars need to look beyond (or below) the Supreme Court and national policy-makers to try to understand politics and law.[34] However, after this wave of research, studies in the political science of criminal justice issues all but disappeared and such research was relegated to criminologists for several decades.

Even as scholars such as Wilson and Dolbeare made exhortations for further study of criminal justice institutions, they ignored one major institution—prisons. Prison studies were the singular domain of sociology scholars who tended to focus on what was happening inside of the walls. These studies assumed as a prerequisite for study that prisons fit solidly into what Erving Goffman would later label "total institutions," those institutions that needed little from the outside world to function.[35] Early prison scholars, such as Donald Clemmer[36] and Gresham Sykes,[37] were far more interested in inmate culture and sociology than any linkages to the outside world. In those few times when these linkages were made, these scholars viewed the prison as a microcosm of the larger society of so-called deviants. There was little interest in thinking about the prison as a political institution, and this first wave of prison research showed no interest in the politics of prisons.[38]

The next major development in the prison literature also focused on inmate behavior but was more interested in the rehabilitative model and its effects or lack thereof as a jumping-off point. These studies all seem to fit into the "what works?" genre of the literature, a way of looking at inmate behavior that continues in criminology fields to this day.[39] This research looks at prison programs to evaluate their impact on recidivism rates. There is some interest in the outside world in these studies, but only insofar as it relates to policy choices for inmate rehabilitation or inmate behavior.

The one major exception to this rule is the work of James Jacobs.[40] Jacobs's groundbreaking study of Stateville prison asked questions about the prison and its role in larger society in a way ignored up until then.[41] Jacobs understood that looking at a prison system as a snapshot in time gave a skewed version of how the prison formed and its impact on the larger society. His deeper insights into the uniqueness of certain prisons and the influences of the prison managers may have made his finding less generalizable, but closer to reality. Prisons for Jacobs were organic creatures with a life of their own.

There has been some work that has tried to place prisons in a social context, most of which has come from poststructuralist scholars, the most famous of which is Michel Foucault's *Discipline & Punish*.[42] Additionally, David Garland's works, *Punishment and Modern Society* and *The Culture of Control* make enticing arguments about political development and the prison.[43] However, Garland's work is primarily interested in the prison writ large, and, of necessity, it does not consider individual institutions.

John DiIulio's work on prison management in *Governing Prisons* shifted the paradigm, but not as much as it might have.[44] DiIullio made prison studies a more comfortable fit for political scientists, not by making more explicit the linkages to the larger political system, but by changing the underlying assumptions made by the "What works?" and other sociological scholars. DiIulio begins from the assumption that the goal of prisons is not to rehabilitate inmates, but to keep the inmates and staff safe. DiIulio researches the effect that prison administrators have on this issue, one of the few scholars since Jacobs to consider prison issues from a standpoint of anyone other than the inmates. In some ways, this question itself fits in with the larger policy questions about the death of the rehabilitative model of corrections, but is not explicitly interested in the larger political context.

In DiIulio's later work, he states his hope that social science research on prisons gains a more explicit link to policy outcomes and the "real world," but in doing so claims that "there is no meaningful body of social science research on corrections."[45] DiIulio argued that policy outcomes and impacts are all but ignored in the prison literature, much to the detriment of current scholarship. Ann Chih Lin's *Reform in the Making* also looks at prisons through a political scientist's lens, but also makes linkages to larger issues about prison programs.[46] She looks at rehabilitation programs as a policy choice, and by looking at actual participation in such programs, evaluates their impact. She finds that the Martinson conclusion that "nothing works" is premature and misguided and that despite many prisons having programs on the books, actual participation in these programs varies greatly.[47] Despite the policy implications of Lin's work, neither she nor DiIulio locate prisons in a larger, overtly political context.

Charles Bright's *The Powers that Punish* is one work that does so.[48] Bright seeks to understand Michigan's Jackson Prison in a particular historical era and places it into the context of the state's politics at the time. Bright's is not a narrative of how politics affects prisons, but instead seeks to understand the interconnectedness of politics and the largest prison in the world at that time. Although Bright makes explicit arguments against generalizing his findings, his method should not be ignored. By looking at one prison over a time period and its relationship to the larger political system, Bright gives an understanding of the prison's role in society in real terms, unlike his more theoretical predecessors. The main problem with Bright's work is that it is essentially a historical account of an era long since past. He studies the era of the big house (in fact, he studies the biggest big house in the country in Jackson Prison) and puts it in its historical place. However, his argument does not foresee the changes the prison system has undergone, from architecture to professionalization to unthinkable expansion, but he does link the prison to other political institutions, most notably the governorship, and as such, his argument is useful.[49]

Unlike Bright's work, most interest in studying prisons and their direct relationship to another political institution has looked at the relationship between the courts and corrections.[50] These books view prisons as a political institution, but one that is subservient to the courts or at least inextricably linked to them. But prisons are a legal and political institution in their own right and are treated as such in this study. Additionally, the lack of interest in prisons is puzzling given the politicization of crime issues more generally and the growing percentage of state budgets earmarked for the building and maintaining of prisons. This book will add to what will hopefully be a growing body of studies that look at criminal justice issues generally through a political lens.

POLITICAL RESPONSIVENESS

The Constitution of 1789 deals mainly with the problems of federalism. At its core, it outlines what powers will be granted to the federal government and what will be retained by the states. The antifederalists, especially Thomas Jefferson, viewed the document as inherently antidemocratic and felt that the closer the power was to the people, the better. He viewed a country held together by a series of small ward republics in which the people would be intimately involved in the daily workings of the government, because a centralized government far away was not responsive enough to the people. Whether or not this is true for all issues, it seems to be so when it comes to who is running a prison system and how it deals with the community in which it is located.

Most of the 200-plus-year history of the Supreme Court is riddled with examples of the difficulty in our constitutional democracy when dealing with questions of federalism and the powers of the different jurisdictions. In fact, many of the most famous cases in the Court's history, from *McCulloch* to *Brown* are, at least in part, about such questions. However, this is not a story of what the various levels of government can or cannot do based on the Constitution or over 200 years as a republic. It is a story about how reactive and responsive those various levels of government are to their citizenry. However, this is not an argument about new federalism; it is about political responsiveness. State prison managers argue that the greater responsiveness to the local community by the prisons was due to the shorter distance between the town and the state Department of Corrections as opposed to the federal BOP.

The issue of governmental responsiveness to its constituency has long been a topic that dominates political science.[51] For our purposes, it will suffice to say that political scientists, especially American political scientists, have often found the issue of the responsiveness of the political system to its constituents a meaningful and fruitful issue to study. Despite this interest in political responsiveness, scholars have shown little interest in multilevel jurisdictional studies. There has been very little interest in comparing the responsiveness of one level of government as compared to another. For the most part, studies of various social movements and agents of policy change focus on one institution or, where more than one institution is involved, those institutions that are at the federal or state level, but not both. Recently, a few studies have looked at policy change in different venues.[52] These studies look at strategies that interest groups use to achieve a policy change. They do so by looking at which levels of government are better forums to be heard. These studies may look at a different question than posed in this book, but they recognize that state and federal institutions have a different level of responsiveness to interest groups, similar to the responsiveness difference to communities in this study.

Unlike state legislatures or Congress, prison officials are not elected and not beholden to any constituency outside of their own bureaucracy. These officials are an administrative arm of the elected branches and those elected officials are a part of the constituency that prison officials serve. In other words, although they are not elected officials themselves, they are beholden to elected officials, although indirectly. But prison officials have become far more political, and prison administrators now must walk the halls of the legislature as well as they walk the tiers of the prison.

The question of why state institutions are more responsive than federal ones is a question that I can only begin to answer, but my hypothesis is that there are three reasons. The first is electoral in that state politicians have more at stake if they alienate a small rural town because it makes up a larger percentage of his or her constituencies. A state politician is much more likely to respond to community concerns in a timely and forceful manner for fear of losing the support of a large percentage of the constituency. The second possibility relates to the distance between the prisons and their home agency. Beeville is 138 road miles from Austin, whereas Florence, Colorado, is 1,700 miles from Washington, D.C., hardly an afternoon's drive. Additionally, there is a regional TDCJ office in Beeville, whereas the regional office in charge of Florence is located in Kansas City, Kansas. This physical distance is obviously less important than it once was, but there are also more levels of bureaucracy to wade through when dealing with the federal government, a bureaucratic distance between facility and home office that is difficult for a community to wade through.

A possible third reason may have more to do with the prison's employees themselves. Federal employees appear to be more aloof, perhaps even more sophisticated (or just more arrogant) than their new rural neighbors. There is a sense of superiority with the federal employees that one does not see with their counterparts who work for the state. The reasons for this sense of superiority are difficult to gauge, but impossible to miss. The community's residents are very aware of it, and from an observational level, it was an issue that I could see as well. At large community gatherings in which they attended, I could easily identify the prison staff by their mode of dress and the way they carried themselves.

Political responsiveness, or lack thereof, is one of the more consistent themes that can be seen in this book. Whether this fits into an inherent problem of federalism or a more specific issue in the prison's culture, what emerges are narratives of a relationship told by three different institutions. These "stories" all focus on the relationship between the prisons and the institutions, but the stories told in Beeville differ greatly from those told in Florence. The next section will discuss the model I used to organize these narrative-prevailing and competing stories.

PREVAILING AND COMPETING STORIES

Charles Bright, in his book *The Powers that Punish*, argues that to understand the relationship between politics and prisons, one must understand the historical narrative viewed from all of the pertinent actors.[53] He says, "[T]he relationship of prisons and politics . . . poses questions that cannot, in my view, be addressed abstractly or normatively; they require a close reading of historical dynamics in a particular time and place."[54] It is in this spirit that this study was undertaken. It attempts to understand the "new" prison town through the eyes of those most involved at a specific time and place to understand the implications of this phenomenon. To do so, I use William Lyons's model of competing and prevailing stories.[55]

In these towns, there is a group of intertwined institutions—the local government, the local police, and the prison. Each of these institutions is located within the power structure and has a claim to the "prevailing story" of the effects of the prison on the community and the relationship among the institutions themselves.[56] For Lyons, the prevailing story is one that is top-down in nature: the one created by the dominant power structure. According to Lyons, "prevailing stories construct history and the present to support state-centered stories."[57] The prevailing story (or perhaps the prevailing myth) that dominates the discourse in both communities in my study is one that comes from the state and federal government, not one created by the local governmental institutions or the prisons themselves. The myth is that the prisons have saved these communities from economic ruin and possibly extinction. The data do not bear this out, but this seems to be beside the point. This myth seems to be taken as fact by many of my respondents, and the state and federal governments are dependent on this myth to continue to find communities that are willing to "give away the store" to land a new prison facility.

Studies may not show any significant economic impact on these communities by the prisons, but there is no way to empirically "prove" or "disprove" the prevailing myth. Put more simply, how can one show what would have happened to these communities had they not landed the prisons? Even studies that compare prison communities to nonprison communities in rural areas cannot claim to do this with any certainty.[58]

Each of the major institutions of power in these communities has a story to tell in this regard. To again borrow terminology from Lyons, these are the "competing stories" of the impact that the prison has had and the relationship that has developed. These stories are the data on which this book is based. But the differences among the stories go beyond just institutional differences and the stories told by the two towns often differ from one another. There is a distinct advantage to this method. As Lyons argues, "[T]his analytical strategy serves as a way of hearing many different voices in the text without granting immediate credibility to any one of them."[59] In doing so, we can begin to see the "discourses" about community and power that serve as an underlying basis for this study.[60]

The competing stories are told in various ways in the communities, but to gain the best perspective, I tell them from each institution's standpoint. For example, the prison officials and community leaders have different stories to tell based on their perspective. In doing so, one is able to see how differently similarly situated actors view the relationship in the two different communities. Using the notion of competing stories to tell the tale of what has gone on is an effective tool for adding to our base of knowledge in this field. These two small rural communities tell similar stories in their desperation to land some institution to save them from economic ruin, but the story they tell of what happens after getting their wish differs greatly.

To tell these stories, each substantive chapter will tell the story from the standpoint of a single institution. By doing so, we can see how the individual institution's relationship in Beeville compares to the same institution in Florence. What emerges are some similarities, but mostly glaring differences that have developed over time. It is in these differences where we begin to see the larger themes of this book develop.

Notwithstanding the above-mentioned pitfalls, this research generates new and potentially fruitful areas of study that may have remained uncovered otherwise. These new areas will be discussed at length in chapter seven after the groundwork is laid in the following four chapters, and the first of these will try and understand these two communities in terms of place and shared social history.

ORGANIZATION OF CHAPTERS

This book seeks to bring together the worlds of politics and prisons in a new way. It is, in many ways, a harkening back to the work of James Q. Wilson[61] and Kenneth Dolbeare[62] in its interest in understanding a criminal justice institution and its relationship to the local political structure. Rather than organizing this like a classic case study and discussing each town separately, I take into account the interpretive nature of the research and at times discuss both communities simultaneously. Despite what can be gleaned from the difference between the two relationships, there is much that they have in common.

Chapter two focuses on methodological issues. As stated above, I found that the blending of two qualitative methods—comparative case study research and a participant-observational methodology—worked best in answering the research questions posed. These two methodologies serve the differing goals of this research well; one that combines impact analysis with an exploratory study of relationships that develop over time between the communities' institutions and the prison.

Chapter three discusses the history and place of these two rural communities. In it, I focus on the lobbying process that landed the prisons in the first place, as well as their distinct geographical and social makeup. Chapter four begins the institutional findings. It looks at the relationship from the standpoint of the prison itself. I argue that the relationship that develops has two influences: whether the prison is state run or federally run and how wardens and the senior prison officials choose to interact with the community. Wardens have a tremendous amount of autonomy in such dealing, and different wardens view this part of their job with great degrees of importance. Although some wardens view community relations as a vital part of their job and act accordingly, some seem to view dealing with the local community as a nuisance that takes them away from the more important job of dealing with issues inside of their facility. This chapter develops the dichotomy between these two types of prison administrators that I have termed "citizens" and "hermits."

Chapter five looks at the relationship that develops afterward from the perspective of the community itself. The community's story is about three major issues. The first two—jobs and housing—develop during the lobbying process when the two sides are trying to sell themselves to the other entity. The last one is about the type of relationship that develops over time and the influence of federalism on that relationship.

Chapter six looks at this issue from the viewpoint of local law enforcement and the courts. Prisons have a larger impact on local law enforcement and courts than on any other part of the local government. They also have the most interaction. Not only do the local police lend prisons their drug-seeking dogs and aid in finding escapees, corrections officers who move to the community sometime run afoul of the law. Prison administrators and law enforcement claim there can be a kinship of sorts that develops between these two groups because they are in similar lines of work. One might hypothesize that in both communities, the police will have a similar story to tell, but they do not. By looking at the issues from the police perspective in both communities, we begin to see the reasons for the differences emerging and the differences between state and federal institutions.

Chapter seven summarizes the findings, offers directions for future research, and outlines some of the broader implications of this study. Even with the slowing in the growth of the prison population, prison building is still on the rise. More and more communities are hosting these facilities, and this makes understanding how the prison, as a legal and political institution, interacts with the community in which it is sited as important as understanding how jobs are created or whether or not local sales tax revenue is on the rise. Because nearly one-third of all counties in the United States now host a prison, this issue is only becoming more important for future study and is not an issue to be ignored. At its base, this book takes this issue seriously by trying to find out what happens when the big house comes to a small town.

NOTES

1. *Ruiz v. Estelle* 679 F.2d 1115, 1126 (1982), cert. denied, 460 U.S. 1042 (1983).

2. According to Bureau of Justice statistics, 2,166,260 people were incarcerated at the end of 2001, approximately 1 in every 143 people or approximately 0.7 percent of the total population. http://www.ojp.usdoj.gov/bjs/pub/pdf/p02.pdf.

If one includes those on probation and parole, 1 in every 32 adults or 3.1% of the population is under some form of criminal justice custody. http://www .ojp.usdoj.gov/bjs/pub/press/ppus02pr.htm.

3. In 1980, the total prison and jail population combined was 503,586. http://www.ojp.usdoj.gov/bjs/glance/tables/corr2tab.htm.

4. Lawrence et al., *The New Landscape of Imprisonment: Mapping America's Prison Expansion*, 8.

5. Their study looked at the 10 states with the largest growth in the numbers of prisons in the 1980s and 1990s.

6. Beale, "Prisons, Population, and Jobs in Nonmetro America."

7. Ostrum, "Converting Threats into Opportunities," 9.

8. McGhee, *Prisons and Politics*. Jacobs, *New Perspectives on Prisons and Imprisonment*. Jacobs, *Statesville: The Penitentiary in Mass Society*. Diulio, *Governing Prisons: A Case Study of Correctional management*. Bright, *The Powers that Punish: Prison and Politics in the Era of the "Big House," 1920–1955*. Lin, *Reform in the Making: The Implementation of Social Policy in Prison*. Gilmore, *Golden Gulag*.

9. For example, according to the 2000 census, Florence had a population of 3,653, whereas the four federal facilities held 3,018 inmates as of September 9, 2006. Inmate data retrieved from http://bop.gov/locations/weekly_report. jsp on September 9, 2006.

10. There are still communities that view prisons as a NIMBY, but because there are enough communities that actually want them, corrections departments no longer seek to site prisons where there is community opposition.

11. Hooks, Mosher, Rotolo, and Lobao. "The Prison Industry: Carceral Expansion and Employment in U.S. Counties, 1969–1994," 57.

12. Florence, Colorado, is currently home to the Federal Corrections Complex–Florence, which houses four separate facilities, including the federal government's only level-six (i.e., highest security) prison. Beeville is now home to three facilities, having added two new facilities (Garza East and West), the TDCJ's classification facilities, and the McConnell unit. The TDCJ's corrections officer training facility is also located in Beeville.

13. Cañon City is Colorado's largest prison town and is home to eight state prison facilities and a local jail. Fremont County has more prisons than any other county in the United States.

14. McShane et al., "Prison Impact Studies: Some Comments on Methodological Rigor." I also agree that there is a value to time series analysis and I intend to do so with the economic statistics, but the purpose of this study is not to see if perceptions have changed over time but on the actual effect.

15. Maxim, "Prisons and Their Perceived Impact on Local Community: A Case Study." McShane et al., "Prison Impact Studies: Some Comments on Methodological Rigor." Thies, *The Big House in a Small Town: The Economic and Social Impacts of a Correctional Facility on its Host Community*. Carlson, "Doing Good and Looking Bad: A Case Study of Prison/Community Relations."

16. Besser et al., "The Development of Last Resort: The Impact of New State Prisons on Small Town Economies." Yanarella and Blankenship, "Big House on the Rural Landscape: Prison Recruitment as a Policy Tool of Local Economic Development." Hooks et al., "The Prison Industry: Carceral Expansion and Employment in U.S. Counties, 1969–1994." King et al., "Big Prisons, Small Towns: Prison Economics in Rural America." Jacobson, *Downsizing Prisons: How to Reduce Crime and End Mass Incarceration.*

17. The exception to this rule are the private prison companies that do pay some property taxes, but tax abatements are often given to these corporations to entice them to locate a prison in a town. I look briefly at the issue of private prison corporations and community relations in chapter seven.

18. As we will see below, this is no small issue because some prisons actually run at nearly 200 percent of capacity, meaning they are essentially paying for only half of the water and other utilities that they use.

19. Jacobs, *Statesville: The Penitentiary in Mass Society.* Jacobs, *New Perspectives on Prisons and Imprisonment.*

20. Carlson, "Doing Good and Looking Bad: A Case Study of Prison/Community Relations." Theis, *The Big House in a Small Town: The Economic and Social Impacts of a Correctional Facility on its Host Community.* Belk, *Making it Plain: Deconstructing the Politics of the American Prison-Industrial Complex.* Gilmore, *Golden Gulag.*

21. Belk, *Making it Plain: Deconstructing the Politics of the American Prison-Industrial Complex.* Belk's study of New York and Virginia does an excellent job of differentiating the politics of the two states to fit it into his larger argument about the prison-industrial complex, but it does not concern itself with any typology of the prisons themselves. The prison as an institution remains outside of the scope of his research, other than as a policy choice that small towns have made for economic development and as a way of creating the so-called prison-industrial complex.

22. DiIulio, *Governing Prisons.* Jacobs, *Statesville: The Penitentiary in Mass Society.* Lin, *Reform in the Making: The Implementation of Social Policy in Prison.*

23. Belk, *Making it Plain: Deconstructing the Politics of the American Prison-Industrial Complex.* Gilmore, *Golden Gulag.*

24. This phenomenon has been well documented, in that the prison population of the United States increased from 319,598 in 1980 to 1,421,911 in 2004. Data retrieved from http://www.ojp.usdoj.gov/bjs/glance/tables/corr2tab.htm on August 22, 2006.

25. Geertz, *Local Knowledge.*

26. The critique of participant-observer research has been quite extensive, but wholly unfair. For example, Robert LeVine points out that "[f]or many academic psychologists, there is a wide gulf between data obtained through the formal methods of empirical science and data obtained through other means, not fully specifiable in advance, which they deride as impressionistic and anecdotal." "Knowledge and Fallibility in Anthropological Field Research." In Brewer and Collins, eds., *Scientific Inquiry in the Social Sciences*, 173.

27. Bureau of Justice Statistics, 2006.

28. Bureau of Justice Statistics, 2004.

29. Jacobson, *Downsizing Prisons: How to Reduce Crime and End Mass Incarceration*.

30. Jacobson, *Downsizing Prisons: How to Reduce Crime and End Mass Incarceration*. Edgerton, *Montana Justice: Power, Punishment, and the Penitentiary*. Dyer, *The Perpetual Prisoner Machine: How America Profits from Crime*. Bright, *The Powers that Punish: Prison and Politics in the Era of the "Big House," 1920–1955*. Mauer and Chesney-Lind, *Invisible Punishment*.

31. Klonoski et al., *The Politics of Local Justice*, 4.

32. Wilson, *The Variety of Police Behavior: The Management of Law and Order in Eight Communities*, 4.

33. Dolbeare, *Trial Courts in Urban Politics*.

34. Heumann, *Plea Bargaining: The Experiences of Prosecutors, Judges and Defense Attorneys*. Klonoski et al., *The Politics of Local Justice*.

35. Goffman, *Asylums*.

36. Clemmer, *The Prison Community*.

37. Sykes, *The Society of Captives: A Study of a Maximum Security Prison*.

38. One could argue that John Irwin and others initiated a new wave of the literature of prisons, but I would argue that they were essentially doing the same research asking different questions. It was still very inmate-focused work with a specific interest in social groups inside of the prison walls. Irwin himself has spawned an interesting subfield of the prison literature, the convict criminology movement. This movement argues, in essence, that one need to have served time to really understand prison social structure. See Ross and Richards, *Convict Criminology*, 2003.

39. Martinson, "What Works? Questions and Answers about Prison Reform." Austin and Irwin, *It's About Time*.

40. Jacobs, *Statesville: The Penitentiary in Mass Society*. Jacobs, *New Perspectives on Prisons and Imprisonment*.

41. Jacobs, *New Perspectives on Prisons and Imprisonment*. In fact, it was Jacobs who first posed one of the questions asked in this book, namely, "What effect does a prison have on a community?"

42. Foucault, *Discipline & Punish: The Birth of the Prison*.

43. Garland, *Punishment and Modern Society*. Garland, *The Culture of Control: Crime and Social Order in Contemporary Society*.

44. DiIulio, "Crime and Punishment in Wisconsin." http://thesconz.wordpress.com/2009/09/22/crime-and-punishment-in-wisconsin/.

45. DiIulio, *No Escape: The Future of American Corrections*, 212. DiIulio's most impassioned discussion of this issue can be seen in chapter six of *No Escape*.

46. Lin, *Reform in the Making: The Implementation of Social Policy in Prison*. Lin's book did come out in 2000, nine years after DiIulio made his critique.

47. Martinson, "What Works? Questions and Answers about Prison Reform." Underlying this argument is a conclusion that DiIulio and I share with Lin. DiIulio found that individual prison administrators matter immensely in what goes on in their individual institutions. Those wardens who push for more focus on these programs often see positive results.

48. Bright, *The Powers that Punish: Prison and Politics in the Era of the "Big House," 1920–1955.* William Lyons's book, *The Politics of Community Policing,* is another book that does an excellent job of linking criminal justice institutions and politics. This work will be discussed more fully below.

49. There have been a few other attempts to link politics and prisons, but they usually fall into the journalistic or quasi-journalistic world. Sasha Abramski's *Hard Time Blues* (2002) and Christian Parenti's *Lockdown America* (1999) are the stars of this category and both are wonderful books, but they lack a scholar's eye for detail. Additionally, Joseph Hallinan's *Going Up the River* (2001) introduced me to Beeville, Texas, specifically and the phenomenon of the new prison town specifically and in some ways inspired this book.

50. Feeley et al., *Judicial Policy-Making and the Modern State: How the Courts Reformed America's Prisons.* DiIulio, "Crime and Punishment in Wisconsin."

51. Dahl, *Who Governs? Democracy and Power in an American City.*

52. Baumgartner et al., *Policy Dynamics.* Holyoke, "Choosing Battlegrounds: Interest Group Lobbying across Multiple Venues." Manna, *School's In: Federalism and the National Education Agenda.* Pralle, *Branching Out and Digging In: Environmental Advocacy and Agenda Setting.* Miller, *The Perils of Federalism.*

53. Bright, Charles. I tend to dislike the term "narrative," because it now is so laden with its own ideological baggage. This is why I borrow the terminology of the story from William Lyons. As he states, "I prefer to use the term *stories* (rather than *narratives, messages,* or *discourses*) because its common language meaning is consistent with my more analytical usage, thereby increasing the accessibility of this text to a broader audience without compromising the clarity of my argument" (p. 7, italics in the original).

54. *Ibid.*, 3.

55. Lyons, *The Politics of Community Policing: Rearranging the Power to Punish.*

56. *Ibid.*, 4.

57. *Ibid.*, 7.

58. Hooks et al., "The Prison Industry: Carceral Expansion and Employment in U.S. Counties, 1969–1994."

59. Lyons, *The Politics of Community Policing: Rearranging the Power to Punish,* 6.

60. I use the notion of discourses about community and power in a way that is similar to Greenhouse et al., in *Law and Community in Three American Towns,* which will be discussed more completely in the following chapter.

61. Wilson, *The Variety of Police Behavior: The Management of Law and Order in Eight Communities.*

62. Dolbeare, *Trial Courts in Urban Politics.*

Chapter Two

Moving In, Walking, and Talking: Gathering Information

In studying this subject we must be content if we attain as high a degree of certainty as the matter of it admits . . . It is a mark of the educated man and a proof of his culture that in every subject he looks for only so much precision as its nature permits.

Aristotle, *Nicomachean Ethics*

I've always admired those reporters who can descend on an area, talk to key people, ask key questions, take samplings of opinions and then set down an orderly report very like a road map. I envy this technique and at the same time do not trust it as a mirror of reality. I feel that there are too many realities. What I set down here is true until someone else passes that way and rearranges the world in his own style.

John Steinbeck, *Travels with Charley*

Warden Joe Gunja is a tall, thin man whose glasses seem reluctant to intrude on his chiseled, soldier's features. He was a military police-man before becoming a corrections officer (CO) at the U.S. Penitentiary (USP) at Leavenworth. He worked his way up through the federal corrections system, did two more "tours" at Leavenworth, moved through Texas, and was promoted to his first warden position in Cumberland, Maryland. He arrived at USP–Florence after the so-called "cowboy scandal" in which a group of COs, calling themselves "The Cowboys," was indicted for abusing inmates. Gunja is a fixer: a man brought in to clean up problems in a facility. Soon after our interview, he was promoted to a regional directorship for the Bureau of Prisons (BOP). He has since retired.

When we discussed the economic impact the prison had on the local community, I thought perhaps he would mention unemployment rates, the number of new residents in the town where his prison is situated, or something along those lines, but I was mistaken. "[T]hat Texaco on the corner of Highways 67 and 115 must make a killing. I stop there all the time on my way home," is the only reference he made.[1] Other than that, he sees little change brought by the prison. He says that very few prison employees live in Florence and the prison does not buy many goods from local businesses.

In talking to the director of the local chamber of commerce, Darrel Lindsay, one gets a completely different perspective. Lindsay says that the Federal Correctional Complex at Florence

> literally revived a town that was doomed to be a ghost town. We had 2,700 people here when the prison decided to come. Our population has doubled. Our water and sewer plants were given badly needed upgrades; probably 10 new businesses opened and four new subdivisions have been or are being built. Thirty-eight percent of the federal employees live in Fremont County. And with the new Summa subdivision and golf course, we expect that number to go up. It's almost like it's too good to be true.[2]

From Darrel Lindsay's perspective, the prisons are almost too good to be true. He, perhaps more than anyone in town, has benefited from them. Two of his children work for the BOP, and he appeared on the TLC television network when they came to town to do a special on the prisons there.

The incongruity is understandable because both men are correct. Lindsay is correct in pointing out the population gains and the new businesses in the community, but these growth indicators could just as easily be attributed to the push the community has made to become a tourist destination (most of the new businesses are kitschy antique stores). Gunja is correct in pointing out that the Texaco station does seem to be thriving because of commuter traffic and that most prison employees do not live in Florence proper.

I encounter a similar problem when I ask the warden how he feels about the locals and their view of BOP employees. I tell him that many community members discuss the federal employees as being generally clannish and unfriendly. Warden Gunja claims he has had the opposite experience: He does not feel fully welcomed in the community, and his son feels like people were very wary of him when he started in the local high school.

Both men are looking at a similar issue from different perspectives, that of a warden of a large federal prison and that of a local business leader. Both perspectives are important, and getting this variety of subjective perspectives is what drives the findings in this book. This book seeks to understand this new phenomenon to discover some of the issues that arise through participant observation. There is a long and rich history of this type of "soaking and poking" in political science, and this work is no different.[3] This research "on the ground" led to the more formal interviews with governmental leaders, prison officials, and police personnel.

This chapter will outline the methodology and framework used in this book. In it, I briefly outline some of the major epistemological debates in qualitative research and justify my use of participant observation to understand the issues in these two post-NIMBY ("not in my backyard") prison towns. This book is, at its core, a work of legal ethnography in which I look at the relationship between legal institutions and the community in which they reside by immersing myself in the culture of that community, and I will discuss the steps I took to do so. In that discussion will be a brief history of the legal ethnography. I argue that this study can be distinguished from other legal ethnographies in its broadening of the classic understanding of the law to include criminal justice institutions.

RESEARCH METHOD

In their seminal work, *Designing Social Inquiry*, King, Keohane, and Verba outline how they believe qualitative research must change to live up to the methodological rigor they desire.[4] Their basic argument is that qualitative research needs to become more like quantitative research with its dependence on the scientific method and hypothesis testing.[5] Although meticulous and important, their argument questions much of what is best about qualitative research in the first place. "Qualitative methodologists . . . point to opportunities to move beyond strict hypothesis testing by engaging in an ongoing refinement of concepts, the iterated fine tuning of hypotheses, and the use of specifically targeted case studies that appear likely to suggest new hypotheses and theoretical ideas."[6] This process of exploratory qualitative research leading to hypothesis and theory generation adds to our understanding of issues that either have not been the subject of much academic interest or discuss an issue that has fundamentally changed in some way.

The topic of this study is of the second kind. Although the literature recognizes a fundamental shift from "prisons as NIMBY" to "prisons as economic savior," recent studies still fall back on the same hypotheses and theories as before, mainly by narrowly focusing on economic indicators or survey data on social perceptions.[7] They serve an important function in studying economic indicators and citizen attitudes but miss some fundamental changes that have occurred on the ground. Even when those studies include more qualitative elements, they seem to fall back on interview questions informed more by works of the past than issues of the present.[8]

There is much to be gained by a more interdisciplinary approach to studies such as this. Academic disciplines are important, but when they are too rigid, they lead to less understanding of certain subjects. However, there are some interdisciplinary works that lead us to a greater and deeper understanding of an issue that can lead to further research and study. An ethnographic study undertaken by a political scientist on a subject that has been mainly the province of the criminology world is just that type of work. This book seeks to take what is best in other disciplines in broadening our understanding of a relatively new phenomenon. By borrowing from several disciplines, this study seeks a broad overview to foster further discussion and future research.

Legal ethnographies, like this one, specifically attempt to understand the culture of the community's relationship with some aspect of law through the perspective presented by the actors themselves. Ethnographic work is interested in collecting a different type of data than other methodologies for a different purpose. As John Flood argues,

> This is not to say that ethnography cannot produce systematic results, but it is not overly concerned with questions of validity and reliability in the conventional way, say, that quantitative approaches are. The research process for ethnography is different from others: it is tentative, multi-textured, open-ended and discursive. It starts from a point of learning and enquiry that recognizes (sic) we know little rather than supposing a state of knowledge which is subject to ex post facto ratification.[9]

This research recognizes that there is a "state of knowledge" about these new prison towns while arguing that the state of knowledge is incomplete. Other than the economic-impact studies, we indeed "know little" about this subject, making it ripe for a more interpretive research method and "thick description" to add to our base of knowledge for future work.[10]

The distinction between "classic" ethnographic work, like that of Geertz, and "legal" ethnographic work is mainly a question of focus. While cultural ethnographic work tends to be more generalized,[11] the legal ethnography has a more specified purpose. This mode of research is certainly not a new undertaking, but in its early incarnation, most legal anthropologists kept their focus abroad.[12] This began to change in the 1980s and 1990s, with the rise of the Law and Society movement, which allowed legal scholars to look for new ways to understand the effects of law on communities and cultures and a forum in which to discuss different methodological strategies. During this time, several scholars conducted ethnographic studies in the United States.[13] However, the focus of the field remained abroad.[14]

Legal ethnographies generally, especially those done in this country, study the individual or the community's relationship to "the law." They attempt to understand how people use (or even view) the law in their lives through their own lens and narrative descriptions. However, in this research, "the law" is fairly narrowly defined and is usually related to courts.[15] Although no scholars explicitly argue that the civil legal system is an exhaustive notion of what law entails, their specific focus implicitly ignores other legal institutions and their relationship to the community. As Greenhouse argues, "along with other legal ethnographers, we felt compelled to reorient our comparative questions around specific problematic aspects of the state of norms and institutions in everyday life."[16] In theory, this may well be true, but the focus of most legal ethnographers remains in the civil courts and on civil litigation. The institutions involved in the criminal justice system, especially cops and corrections (if you'll excuse the alliteration), are also legal institutions. The last of these, corrections, is rarely treated as a legal institution and even more rarely as a political one.[17] I argue that it is both.

By looking at prisons as a political institution, we can look at institutional relationships rather than treating prisons as what Erving Goffman has termed a "total institution," a closed society that needs little from the institutions that surround it.[18] Although this may have been true in the past, the shifting nature of prisons in our society as well as the booming prison population has brought prisons more into the light of day.[19] They have become political entities and have developed institutional relationships.[20] Prisons have become a more visible part of our daily lives in many ways, leading to more interest in what is going on behind the razor wire. MSNBC's series *Lockup* and similar shows on the National Geographic network have given the general public a glimpse of what happens inside of prisons. Corrections budgets nationwide have exploded, despite tightening state budgets, and taxpayers are interested in where the money is going. Prisons are now an important part of our political world and should be viewed as a political institution rather than just an arm of the criminal justice system.

In recognizing this shift, this work begins to give a more complete understanding of the new prison towns by looking into areas that other scholars have overlooked. It is exploratory and seeks to go beyond what can be understood by surveys or interview data alone. However, there are significant interview data in my research. I conducted 62 formal interviews with local governmental officials and prison managers as well as local business and educational leaders. But this research went beyond just the formal interview process. I conducted over 100 informal interviews with community residents and prison employees. I attended city council meetings, community relations board meetings, and local economic development corporation meetings. I spent time in six local prisons. I essentially sought to immerse myself in the two towns in my study.

To facilitate this immersion into the community, I purchased a 19-foot travel trailer that became my home for over a year. I spent six months living in a trailer park on the outskirts of Beeville and eight months over two summers living in Florence. This experience gave me insights and experiences that I might not have enjoyed had I stayed in a hotel or just visited in short stints. As I walked my dog through the trailer park and town, I would start conversations with local community members, and these informal "interviews" led to a wealth of information. The respondents invariably asked what I was doing in their community, which I used as my opening to begin to ask questions. I would answer that I was studying the relationship between the prison and the town, and that I was writing a book about the subject.

This opener led in many different directions. I always brought up three issues: the effect the prison has had, the relationship between the town and prison, and what specifically had changed. Otherwise, I was willing to let the conversations wander in various directions. I never took notes during these sessions for one major reason: I very quickly noticed how nervous it made people. My goal was to make these meetings as informal as possible and note taking was not always conducive to this. Given this, I directly quote very few people with whom I had informal interviews.[21] I feel that what was lost by this method is far outweighed by the amount of "insider" information I was given along the way, whether it was the teen that showed me how to pick out the trailers where methamphetamines were being cooked by feeling for heat or the ex-inmate who told me about living under supermax conditions in a Colorado prison. Although information like this may appear to be tangential to my study, allowing the residents of these communities to let me into their lives in whatever way they wished helped me to gain a better understanding of life there.

In many ways, this is as much a book about rural America and its struggles as it is about prisons and communities. The decision to lobby for the prisons is the Faustian bargain these communities have made to survive. Rural communities across the country go through the same struggles to find jobs and economic growth strategies whether they have lobbied for prisons or not. Florence and Beeville are just two communities that, like many other communities, have made their choices and hooked their wagon to the prison-industrial complex.

In the spirit of gaining a better understanding of the towns as a whole, I spent endless mornings in local coffee shops and spent afternoons in the mayor of Beeville's barbershop. I watched the Saturday night ritual of "cruising" in Florence and talked to the teenagers who drove endlessly around Main Street that night. I had a parolee point out what businesses he claimed were selling drugs out of the back door and even taught a class at a local community college. I spent several days shadowing the Bee County sheriff as he went about his routine. In other words, I tried to understand the fabric of these towns and, as much as possible, become an insider.

This process is not simple or easy. As one scholar argues, "[E]thnography presents a unique set of problems for the researcher, in part because it is a messy process. There are problems of entry, developing trust and empathy, recording interaction, and making sense of ethnographic data."[22] In my research, "problems of entry" were solved by an informal strategy. For example, gaining access to prisons is not an easy task,[23] and I went through informal channels, rather than formal ones, using people I met and interviewed along the way to gain access to prison officials.[24] I was surprised by how much access I was given at times and how easy it was, especially in Texas.[25] I found that, for me, introducing myself to local officials and community members in person at meetings or even in coffee shops was more effective than any other way of gaining access.

I followed a similar procedure in each community to begin the process. Before I "hit the road," I gathered as much information as I could about the local prisons, but I tried to learn very little about the town itself beyond the basics of how they fit into my study. I wanted, as much as possible, to learn about the town from the people who lived there. This book is their story from their view as much as possible and filtered through my lens.

My feelings upon entering both communities were a mixture of relief and exhaustion. Both towns required several days of driving with my travel trailer in tow, a nerve-racking experience for an RV novice like myself. My first stop, after setting up at the trailer park, was the local library.[26] Neither town's local newspaper was easily accessible from elsewhere, so this was my first priority—to put together a history of the prisons in town from a local perspective and the process through which they were sited.[27] I used these newspapers as my first glimpse into the history I would later get from the people in the town.

My second stop was the local community college. In Florence, I did this solely to get Internet access (my trailer was not exactly wired for e-mail), but I found that the employees there were a good resource. They had an understanding of my project, and the vice president at the time was incredibly supportive and actually hired me to teach a class. After that, I went about getting to know the community and its residents. I spent several weeks in each community "soaking and poking" without starting any formal interviews. I became a fixture in the local coffee shops and generally made a nuisance of myself around town, talking to whoever did not ignore me or look at me like I was crazy for interrupting their coffee drinking and cinnamon roll eating. I wanted to get the average resident's perspective before speaking to anyone in a position of power. I wanted the citizens to help me develop my interview questions and try to ask about those issues that concerned them as residents, not the questions that I thought were important coming in from the outside. I continued to check myself with community residents throughout the process and get feedback on my interviews with community elites. I always enjoyed discussing my interviews with people I got to know well and hearing their view of the responses, be it a "Yeah, she has that right" or "Oh my God, he is so full of crap." It kept me centered and interested in digging deeper into the issues that were raised, always remembering that politicians, whether in Washington, D.C., or Beeville, Texas, often have an agenda that they are putting forward.

It was at this point where the paths diverged. In any attempt to gain access to elites, even in a small town, the road can often be made easier through the help of someone on the inside. I was fortunate enough to find such a person in both communities. In Florence, it was the college vice president who was my "in" to the prisons and community leaders; in Beeville, it was the prison prosecutor who did so. Both people let me do an enormous amount of "hanging around," putting up with my incessant questions and requests to tag along with them to meetings.[28] They would introduce me to everyone we met and also made phone calls on my behalf. In both towns, those people I did not meet in this manner, I met at city council meetings and in Beeville, at the county commissioner's court. There were very few outsiders at these meetings, especially a nonlocal sitting in the back and taking notes, so it was not difficult to get attention and introduce myself afterward.

My formal interviews were structured around several questions that I asked every interviewee. These included questions about how the prison came to town and what their perceptions of the effects of the prison were.[29] From there, I let the conversation flow. I wanted to have systematic answers to certain questions, but I was willing to allow for a fair amount of wandering. For the most part, this was not a problem. Before I would ask my first formal questions, I always warmed up my respondents by asking about their work. When I did not do this, I often got very brief answers to the questions that I asked, which were answered in detail by others. I wanted to build rapport before asking the more important questions.[30] For the most part this worked, and 30-minute appointments rarely lasted less than an hour and often lasted longer.[31]

With town officials, I always let them tell me their version of how the prisons came to town. This could sometimes be very repetitive, but the subtle (and sometimes not-so-subtle) differences in the stories, or even those details emphasized by one person over another, were important in the social history discussed in the next chapter. I tried my best to always act like this was the first time I had heard the story, sometimes asking follow-up questions aimed at completing my understanding of the process.[32]

I made an attempt to interview all local elected officials. For the most part, I did so, and those who I did not interview were the result of scheduling conflicts, rather than a refusal on their part to speak to me. I interviewed both town's city managers and a few former ones. I also interviewed the heads of both local chambers of commerce as well as police chiefs, sheriffs, and as many of their underlings as they would allow.

Some respondents who were formally interviewed in one place were not necessarily in the other. For example, I spoke to the superintendent of the Beeville school system, who referred me to a principal of the elementary school where many children of COs went. She was extremely helpful in discussing some of the issues involved with this influx of children to the school system. Given how few COs actually live in Florence or have children who attend the schools there, this hardly seemed a necessary interview to conduct there.

There were also other community leaders who had no equivalent person from one place to the other; for example, the special prison prosecutor. There is no prison prosecutor in Florence and even the district attorney was of little help with prison prosecutions because they were tried in federal court. I also spoke with several local judges in Beeville, but I did not try to interview the federal judges who were responsible for Florence because they were located a distance away in Pueblo. Overall, there were very few interviews that I wish I had conducted that I did not and few community leaders who did not give graciously of their time.

On the prison's side, I attempted to interview all of the top officials in both states. This was a far easier task in Texas than in Colorado. Every person I contacted in Texas was willing to meet with me (including several former wardens and one warden who had moved to a facility in Huntsville, Texas), and I was rarely made to feel like I was intruding on an interviewee's time. I spoke to the current wardens and assistant wardens of all three facilities in Beeville as well as several majors—the highest uniformed officers in the Texas Department of Criminal Justice (TDCJ). Even the regional director of the TDCJ and director of institutions for all of Texas met with me.

This process was not as easy in Colorado. Several wardens granted me interviews after I met them and introduced myself at a local economic development corporation luncheon, but several others refused outright or ducked my calls after I met them. Even so, I formally interviewed seven top administrators for the BOP and spoke to several others informally at various meetings. Those wardens who did meet with me were also extremely courteous and willing to answer questions. One even went so far as to come to my class and give my students a personal tour of his facility.

During the interview process, I realized very quickly that I got much more detailed answers if I began by discussing the job of being a warden or prison administrator rather than beginning with my formal questions. Several administrators wanted to conduct their interviews on the run, giving me a tour of the facility while answering my questions. Although this sometimes led to some interesting incidents, it also led to a much freer-flowing conversation.[33] In every case but one, these very busy individuals went well beyond the time that they scheduled for me.

Most of my interview questions and theories came from the in-depth conversations I had with community residents, very few of which are cited in this study. They gave me the canvas on which my other respondents painted. Often, it was in these encounters and conversations in which I first heard about issues that I discussed at length with prison officials and community leaders. Without the groundwork, these issues never would have come to the surface and I would not have known their importance.

CONCLUSIONS

Exploratory research as a whole is a useful tool in beginning to understand issues and questions when the current state of knowledge is limited. The relationship between prisons and communities is one of these areas of interest. Despite some work in the field, little is known about what these communities can expect to get from these institutions on which they have hung their economic future. These expectations include the economic effects, but the relationship that is developed between the local governmental institutions and the prisons is important as well.

This chapter discussed the method used in this book to expand our knowledge in this field. Like many ethnographic works, it is exploratory. The design involved studying two communities for a substantial period of time to learn the central themes that surface in these new prison towns. The preliminary stages of the research were mainly informal interviews with community residents. I then conducted formal interviews with community and prison leaders about the subjects discussed in the first stage in this research. Using this methodology, I was able to uncover many issues that were not previously discussed in the research on prison towns. However, before discussing these findings, we must first get a better understanding of the towns themselves. The following chapter paints such a picture by detailing the history and geography of Florence and Beeville.

NOTES

1. Gunja, personal communication, July 2003.

2. Lindsay, personal communication, July 2003.

3. In his seminal work *Home Style*, Richard Fenno argued that, "[r]esearch based on participant observation is likely to have an exploratory emphasis." This work draws on a long tradition in political science that, although most famously done by Fenno, has many denizens, especially those who study law, courts, and criminal justice (see Heumann, *Plea Bargaining: The Experiences of Prosecutors, Judges and Defense Attorneys*. Wilson, *The Variety of Police Behavior: The Management of Law and Order in Eight Communities*. Lin, *Reform in the Making: The Implementation of Social Policy in Prison*.

4. King et al., *Designing Social Inquiry: Scientific Inference in Qualitative Research*.

5. For a more complete summary and critique of *Designing Social Inquiry*, see Collier et al., *Rethinking Social Inquiry: Diverse Tools, Shared Standards*.

6. Geraldo Munck in Collier et al., *Rethinking Social Inquiry: Diverse Tools, Shared Standards*, 119.

7. Huling, "Building a Prison Economy in Rural America" in *Invisible Punishment: The Collateral Consequences of Mass Imprisonment*. King et al., "Big Prisons, Small Towns: Prison Economics in Rural America." Besser et al., "The Development of Last Resort: The Impact of New State Prisons on Small Town Economies." Hooks et al., "The Prison Industry: Carceral Expansion and Employment in U.S. Counties, 1969–1994."

8. Thies, *The Big House in a Small Town: The Economic and Social Impacts of a Correctional Facility on its Host Community*. Belk, *Making it Plain: Deconstructing the Politics of the American Prison-Industrial Complex*.

9. In Banakar and Travers, eds., *Theory and Method in Socio-Legal Research*.

10. Geertz, *Local Knowledge: Further Essays in Interpretive Anthropology*.

11. Much of recent ethnographic work tends to be more focused than the more grand ethnographies of the past, so perhaps legal ethnographies are just

a further sectioning off of knowledge. This seems to be the general trend in the social sciences and humanities as a whole, with the larger, more broadly minded studies of the 1970s being replaced by more and more specificity and specialty.

12. Malinowski, *Crime and Custom in Savage Society*. Llewellyn et al., *The Cheyenne Way: Conflict and Case Law in Primitive Jurisprudence*. Bohannan, *Justice and Judgment among the Tiv*. Gluckman, *The Judicial Process among the Barotse of Northern Rhodesia*. Gluckman, *The Ideas in Barotse Jurisprudence*.

13. Merry, *Getting Justice and Getting Even: Legal Consciousness among Working-Class Americans*. Conley, et al., *Rules versus Relationships: The Ethnography of Legal Discourse*. Greenhouse, *Praying for Justice*. Nader, "Controlling Processes in the Practice of Law: Hierarchy and Pacification in the Movement to Reform Dispute Ideology."

14. Moore, "Certainties Undone: Fifty Turbulent Years of Legal Anthropology, 1949–1999."

15. Conley et al., *Rules versus Relationships: The Ethnography of Legal Discourse*. Nader, "Controlling Processes in the Practice of Law: Hierarchy and Pacification in the Movement to Reform Dispute Ideology." Greenhouse et al., *Law and Community in Three American Towns*.

16. *Ibid.*, 9.

17. Charles Bright's *The Powers that Punish* (1996) is one exception to this. There has been ethnographic work done inside prisons (Sykes, *The Society of Captives: A Study of a Maximum Security Prison*. Jacobs, *Statesville: The Penitentiary in Mass Society*. Fleischer, *Warehousing Violence*), but of these works, only Jacobs sees the importance of linking the prison with the outside world.

18. Goffman, *Asylums*.

19. There are many reasons for this shift that will be discussed in chapter five.

20. Bright, *The Powers that Punish: Prison and Politics in the Era of the "Big House," 1920–1955*.

21. Several scholars have discussed the accuracy of their notes when taken after an interview and their use of quotations despite the time lag between comments being made and recorded (Fenno, *Home Style: House Members in Their Districts*. Lin, *Reform in the Making: The Implementation of Social Policy in Prison*). I was not as comfortable with my own memory, so I chose not to use direct quotations in many cases.

22. In Banakar and Travers, eds., *Theory and Method in Socio-Legal Research*, 40.

23. For various descriptions of how scholars get access to prison systems, see DiIulio, *Governing Prisons: A Case Study of Correctional Management*. Jacobs, *Statesville: The Penitentiary in Mass Society*. Fleischer, *Warehousing Violence*. Lin, *Reform in the Making: The Implementation of Social Policy in Prison*.

24. At one point, I tried to go through official channels to gain access to prison employees in Arizona. I was not denied access, per se, but was completely

ignored, even when I showed up at the Arizona Department of Corrections in Phoenix.

25. I believe that Texas's historical battles with the courts helped me in this regard because monitors often inspected the units and many books and studies have been done on the Texas prison system.

26. Florence's library is very limited in resources and in the hours it was open, so I instead used the library facilities in next-door Cañon City, where they have a wonderful local history office. The women who work in the basement office were helpful beyond my wildest dreams, because they spent much of their time cutting and sorting articles from the local papers and filing them by topic.

27. In using local newspapers rather than regional ones, I feel that I was able to discern a more "local" view of the process.

28. See the introduction to *Home Style* for the importance of "hanging around," especially in the early stages of this type of research. Fenno, *Home Style: House Members in Their Districts.*

29. On one occasion, this perception question almost shut down the interview when the respondent said, "You know, I see a lot more lesbians and transvestites hanging around downtown." To this day, I'm not sure if the person was playing with me or answering my question seriously. Either way, I could not figure out where to take the conversation from there.

30. For the importance of building rapport, see Fenno, *Home Style: House Members in Their Districts*, 263–274.

31. However, this did not always happen. Several respondents, especially prison employees, remained guarded throughout my interview and could not wait to get me out of their offices. I would sometimes fall back on some form of "I'm not a reporter here . . . I'm not trying to make you look stupid," with mixed results.

32. I also tried my best to play what Ray Charles referred to as "country dumb," often using stories of my childhood in rural Maine to warm up the conversations. In her article on elite interviewing, Beth Leech makes the argument that one never wants to try and come off as smarter than the interviewee. In rural communities, there also seemed to be a distrust of my being from what they considered an elite eastern university (I am pretty sure by the reaction I got to stating that I was a student at Rutgers that most people had Rutgers confused with Princeton). I found that by mentioning that I grew up in a small town northern Maine helped with this.

33. Two incidents in particular are worth repeating. During one tour/interview, the warden I was interviewing introduced me to an inmate, something no one else did. After meeting this inmate, the warden told me that he had first met this man over 20 years earlier when he was a CO in Texas. He was now a warden in a federal facility and had run into this man in his prison, some 1,000 miles away from their first meeting. A second incident occurred when

a different warden invited me to lunch. I have read many prison memoirs, and a common theme in these books is that inmates will often violate the food served in the staff dining hall with various bodily fluids. I wanted to refuse this gesture, but I felt that I could not without ruining my rapport with this man, so with great trepidation, I ate hot dogs and fries in the staff cafeteria. To date, I have not shown any signs of illness.

Chapter Three

History and Geography

"[C]ommunity" not only conceptually distinguishes the past from the present, but also authentic members of the community from a host of "others" whose presence is perceived to be undermining in any number of ways.

Greenhouse et al., *Law and Community in Three American Towns*

As I drove west on Highway 50 into Fremont County, Colorado, at 8:00 P.M. on a night in June of 2003, I was not expecting to see much. I figured that I would find a home for the night and explore the area the next day. But in the distance, I saw the unmistakable orange glow of the "night" lights of a rather large prison complex. This was my first time actually seeing the lights of ADX Florence, the so-called "Alcatraz of the Rockies," the federal government's only supermax prison. This is where it houses "the worst of the worst" inmates under 23-hour-a-day lockdown. At least I assumed it was ADX Florence. Actually, I was not sure which of the 13 prisons that Fremont County houses I was seeing. My assumption had been that I might catch a glimpse of the ADX from the road, but it could not have been more than a few more seconds before I saw another orange glow, and then another, and then another, and then a billboard for the Colorado Territorial Prison Museum. It might as well have said, "Welcome to Prisontown, USA."

Florence, Colorado, is located where the high eastern plains of Colorado meet the "foothills" of the Rocky Mountains in central Colorado. "Foothills" is a relative term here because these hills are over 9,000 feet high, rising 4,000 feet from the Colorado Plateau below. However, they are foothills when compared to the 13,000- and 14,000-foot peaks of the Sangre de Cristo Mountains to the south and west. Florence has only two stoplights, two motels, and one fast-food joint. It is a town of trailer parks and manufactured houses, with some more stately homes sprinkled in. If it were not for the prisons on the outskirts of town, it would be indistinguishable from hundreds of rural towns throughout the Mountain West.

Beeville, Texas, lies in the heart of South Texas and presents itself quite differently than Florence. Although one can see for miles on a Colorado highway, South Texas is flat: like Kansas flat, really flat and really brown. Driving into Beeville from East Texas, it feels like you might fall off the edge of the Earth at any moment. The roads are long, straight, and seemingly endless. In fact, I was told that the stretch of highway that runs near Beeville to Corpus Christi is the longest stretch of highway without a curve in the United States. Unlike Florence, you could almost trip over the prisons in town without noticing them beforehand.

Texas is only considered a coherent whole by those who do not live there. For Texans, there is a significant cultural distinction based on geography and terrain. East Texas, with Houston as its hub, has more in common with its Louisiana neighbors than it does with the ranchlands of West Texas that former President Bush calls home. South Texas is also distinct. Its culture and demographic makeup has a distinctly Mexican feel to it, and although Beeville is not directly on the border like Laredo or Brownsville, the influence is still obvious. Although Beeville is only a few hours' drive from the urban, cultural centers of San Antonio and Austin, there is nothing cosmopolitan about this place.

There is more to a community than just where it is located. Because ethnographic work is imbedded in the local community, the logical starting point for any study of this type is an understanding of history and geography. Merging together these two distinct places into one study has its problems, so to try to avoid some of these, I begin the substantive chapters by outlining what is distinct about these, two places and discussing some of what they have in common. This chapter will outline the history and geography of these two communities, especially their successful efforts to land a prison.

WHAT IS A COMMUNITY?

The term "community" that is used consistently by the respondents in this study can be troubling and raises many questions. For example, what are the definitional limits of "community?" Is this a question of geography or something deeper? Who is to be considered a part of the community? It is in attempting to answer these questions that the insider/outsider dichotomy begins to take form. The community is defined, in many ways, by who is considered an "insider" and who is considered an "outsider." Geography is part of what matters in this definition, but one is not considered part of a community just on the basis of a geographic location. In many ways, insider status is a self-definition and can be a very fuzzy concept, but it is an important one for the residents of a town. Greenhouse and others argue that the insider or "good" citizen defines himself and others in juxtaposition to the outsider or "bad" citizen and builds important notions about community using this classification.[1]

Defining the insider and outsider is a difficult task. "[T]he boundary between 'insiders' and 'outsiders' is selective, fluid, somewhat arbitrary, and sometimes non-existent. That is, the concept of outsider does not necessarily apply to any actual group."[2] The outsiders in my research often come in the form of newcomers to the community, brought in with the new businesses for economic development purposes. All communities struggle with the encroachment of the larger society on their smaller world, usually because of market forces. Adjustments are made, but many "insiders" consider these changes to be detrimental to their notions of a good community and many have an especially hard time adjusting to new realities and get caught up in the quagmire of economic development policy. On the one hand, a small town saves itself from potential extinction by bringing in new business, but on the other, a new element is brought in that changes the face of the community, bringing in the consummate outsider in the form of new employees.[3]

The outsiders, in the case of the prison, are of a different sort when the new business is a prison. Corrections officers (COs), like other peace officers, are remarkably cliquish. As we will see in chapter five, this is even more noticeable with federal COs. Although the "not in my back yard," "NIMBY"-based literature on prison towns assumes that the outsiders will be so-called "camp followers," families of incarcerated inmates who move to an area to be closer to a loved one, there are little data that bear this out. Families tend not to move to these new prison towns in large numbers and do not become a problematic addition to the community. COs and their families do have a great impact and can change the face of a small town.

In small towns, the idea of community is given "great cultural weight borne by images of a harmonious small town, a face-to-face society."[4] This idea comes from a mix of local social history and personal memory in which there is a harkening back to a local "golden age"; a time "when things worked."[5] The reality of life cannot live up to this mythology, and many bemoan the current state of community in their towns. This is the "myth of community," one that exists in many rural towns. It is the idea that, although there is no community now, but there was a time when it was a part of their lives. Because of this harkening back, there is an important relationship between community and "history" in these small towns. A shared social history is an important part in keeping the myth of community alive; it is a tricky concept and perspectives (as well as one's own "reality") change over time.

There is a tension that specifically arises between the importance of social harmony and the introduction of market realities. The sense in the community is that to simply survive, an influx of new capital is needed and there is inevitably the arrival of an outside element, which in turn brings dissonance into the previous sense of harmony. But this sense of former harmony itself may just be a myth. Nonetheless, the addition of new residents or even commuters becomes the "other" that a community can blame for the current problems. Insiders place these others into a category outside of their community despite the difficulty insiders have in defining exactly what they mean when they use the term.

In other words, there is a bit of myth making, for lack of a better term, at work here. This mythology holds that there was a time when life in Florence or Beeville was ideal, with few problems and great harmony. This is not uncommon (just ask someone over 70 about the 1950s and you are unlikely to hear about Jim Crow laws, and more likely to hear about an idyllic world), but in prison communities, there is a major institution that can be blamed when things go wrong. It is easy to say that issues in town are a result of the prison, which is something I heard a lot in my travels. If life in town is imperfect, it must be the fault of the prison and its employees. If the community was better and stronger in some distant time and memory, the change must have occurred because the prison came to town.

Community becomes a mix of the concepts of geography and a shared social history. This definition automatically and purposely excludes new residents who may move to a town. Their exclusion from and perspective on the community in which they now work is an important one and is better served by keeping them as outsiders.

This is also done because the people who consider themselves insiders do so. Even with this definition, such as it is, the definitional problems continue. The next section will define one of the important parts of the definition of community itself, that of geography.

GEOGRAPHY

If there is such a thing as a quaint rural town, neither Beeville nor Florence is it. Florence has some distinct geographical features that might make it more appealing than Beeville, but it is hardly Vail or Aspen, which lie in the mountains several hours to the north. The poverty of both communities is tangible and obvious to any visitor, with their abundant trailer parks and teenage girls pushing baby carriages. There are no high-end stores in either place or a mall within 30 miles.

Beeville, for its small population size, is actually quite sprawling. There is a downtown area, which has the courthouse and the library at its center, but most of the shopping has moved to the north side of town. This is the commercial zone, with all of the larger stores, except for the large H-E-B grocery store that is on the western edge of downtown. There is a Wal-Mart (which has since become a Super Wal-Mart), a large tractor supply store, and a few fast-food joints and motels. The prisons are on the outskirts of town to the south and east.

Before the prisons came to town, Beeville had been dependent on the military and oil for its subsistence. The first oil well was discovered in Bee County in the late 1920s, and the area saw a small boom, like much of South Texas. Chase Field was commissioned in 1943 as a naval auxiliary station. These two industries were the foundation of Beeville's economy for the middle part of the 20th century. Oil production reached its peak in the 1970s, and Chase Field became smaller through the 1980s until it closed in 1993. Despite these economic engines, Beeville does not lie on an interstate highway (Route 181 is four lanes through town, but a two-lane road for most of the way from Kenedy, Texas, to Mathis). The Southern Pacific Railroad ran through town during the boom era, but it stopped service in 1994, and the tracks have been pulled up.

Florence is much smaller and more compact. Other than a new grocery store and a Super 8 motel (which is a stone's throw from the prisons), there is no commercial life beyond downtown, and downtown itself has little commercial activity aimed at its residents other than the local bars. Florence's residential zones are dilapidated older houses or newer modular homes. The only real growth that is immediately discernable is the new high school, built thanks to a bond issue on the ballot a few years ago. If a resident of Florence wants consumer goods other than food, he needs to go six miles west to Cañon City or 30 miles east to Pueblo. The only clothing store in town closed while I was there, and although the local Super Foods just expanded, it still cannot compete with the Super Wal-Mart in Cañon City.

Unlike Beeville, Fremont County, home to Florence, has always depended on prisons for subsistence. The first territorial prison was built in next-door Cañon City in 1871. Florence never had much industry of its own and has always been dependent on Cañon City for many of its jobs. As Cañon City and the Royal Gorge have become more of a tourist destination, Florence still fights for the economic table scraps. It lies a few miles from Highway 50 and has no regular rail service. Like much of rural America, it struggles just to get by.

To the outside observer, neither community looks like it has experienced an economic boom since the prisons came to town. In rural communities, it seems that the storefronts in downtown are one measure by which locals gauge the strength of their community—the fewer empty storefronts that exist, the healthier the town must be. There is an economic reality at play in this, and more stores might mean a bustling economy, but there is also a symbolic meaning. Many of the individuals who I talked to in both communities discussed the prevalence of empty storefronts in downtown before the prisons came. The empty storefront represents not only a loss of economic security, but also a sense of community instability.

Both towns have filled most of their empty storefronts, but with very different results. The *San Antonio Express* wrote a story about downtown Beeville, stating "while Beeville now has an abundance of fast-food franchises, its newer businesses also include rent-to-own furniture stores, nine signature lenders, three pawn shops and a growing number of payday lenders, including two located in Circle K stores."[6] These are not the kind of stores that most communities crave. They are stores that cater to a constituency living from paycheck to paycheck without enough expendable income to afford luxury items. The situation was much the same as when I was there. Despite this, the H-E-B supermarket has expanded twice since the prisons came, and business at the Wal-Mart is bustling. But this has done little to revitalize downtown.

Main Street in Florence seems to deal in two major commodities— alcohol and antiques. According to local residents, much of Florence's economy is underground, with methamphetamine use quite high among local residents. Meth has done its damage in Florence, much like the rest of the Mountain West, with little relief in sight.[7] Whether or not the bars have opened in response to the prison is questionable, but the antique shops were certainly brought in through other means. According to former city manager Steve Rabe, the Florence business leaders have taken the lead in changing their economic situation with the town's new emphasis on selling antiques and knickknacks because the prisons did not bring the kind of boom they had hoped for. Another former town manager also sees very little change in the economics of Florence that came from the prisons but has seen some growth through other means. The town's business leaders had expected that the government would spend more money in the town on supplies, but the Bureau of Prisons (BOP) has contracts with big firms for almost everything they buy. BOP regulations allow each facility to contract on its own for many of its supplies, but Florence's business leaders rarely get the contracts.[8]

One local warden claims that this is a problem of expectations from the town's standpoint. He said, "they didn't seem to understand that everything we buy has to be bid on and we always buy from the lowest bidder. If the local True Value store is selling hammers for $50 and we can get it elsewhere for $25, we're going to buy the hammer for $25." The point is valid because a large prison facility is not going to shop at the local grocery or department store. Larry Lasha, former Florence town manager, told me that several years ago, a group of business owners had a meeting with the wardens at the Federal Correctional Complex to discuss the possibility of the prisons conducting more business with local vendors, but it seems to have little impact.

Additionally, neither town is a geographical dream world. Despite having mountains at its outskirts, Florence is by no means a beautiful location and is much more arid desert than forest. The mountains might be considered lovely in another setting, but not when one can drive an hour away and see the craggy peaks of the Sangre de Cristos. I heard Florence residents call their mountains "ugly." Even so, at least they have their ugly mountains, because Beeville does not even have a physical feature that is distinctive at all. Not that either town is particularly distinctive. They both look like hundreds of small rural communities around the United States with their dilapidated downtowns and bustling Wal-Marts. Even the prisons do not detract from their rural American appearance, and given the addition of prisons in so many communities, they may actually add to it. Where these two towns differ most is in their social makeup and specifically their racial makeup.

SOCIOECONOMIC FACTORS

In most measures of economic health, Beeville and Florence are very similar when compared to how far behind they are to their respective states and the country as a whole. However, where they diverge is in the changes in median household income levels and unemployment rates, because Beeville's economic indicators have worsened since 1990, whereas Florence's have shown some improvement. This may be a sign that Florence is seeing some positive development due to the prisons, but several scholars point out that these indicators are complex when only looking at a few communities.[9]

The median family income in Beeville in 2000 was $14,000 less than in all of Texas, whereas Florence lagged behind the rest of Colorado at the time by almost $18,000.[10] Both towns lagged behind the country as a whole by almost $16,000 per year. When one considers the relationship between median household incomes in the towns in relationship to the state, these two towns appear to be going in opposite directions between 1990 and 2000. The median household income in Florence was 53 percent that of Colorado as a whole in 1990 but went up to 61 percent in 2000. Beeville's median household income in relation to the rest of Texas has gone down over the same period, from 72 to 65 percent. In Beeville's case, this may not have any relationship to the opening of the prison because the local Naval Air Station also closed during that period of time, with a loss of many jobs. It may be argued that this decline would have been even more severe had the prisons not opened. For Florence, these numbers seem to indicate some growth in relation to the state as a whole and may show that the prisons have indeed had an impact on the economy. However, there may also be something to the argument made by several former city managers that a focus on tourism and the addition of the antique stores to the downtown area has made a difference in Florence's economic health.

Whether or not there has been some growth in Florence, we still have two communities who lag far behind the rest of the country on most measures of socioeconomic status. Although the country as a whole had 9.2 percent of families living below the poverty level in 2000, those numbers were 12.5 and 26.5 percent for Florence and Beeville, respectively. Thirty-three percent of the population as a whole is in professional, managerial, or other related occupations, whereas only approximately 25 percent of the populations of Florence and Beeville are. Neither of these indicators has changed significantly since the prisons came to town, so the growth may come from elsewhere.

Another area of divergence was in unemployment, in which Florence had only a 1.3 percent unemployment rate in 2000 as compared to 5.5 percent in Beeville and 3.7 percent nationally. In the unemployment realm, we again see two towns going in opposite directions since the prisons opened. Beeville's unemployment rate was 3.0 percent in 1990 whereas Florence's was 10.1 percent. The national average in 1990, was 5.6 percent. One might argue that this too is a result of the prisons, but most people, whether from the prison or the community, claim that very few prison jobs went to Florence residents.

In addition to hard economic data, there are other important social indicators. One such indicator is racial, but the racial makeup of the two communities is important for different reasons for the purposes of this study. In Florence, there are a significant number of minority prison workers, most of whom live elsewhere. Part of this reason may be just how white Florence is.[11] According to the 2000 Census, Florence is nearly 93 percent white, with an African American population of 0.3 percent. In other words, Florence has 11 black residents out of a population of 3,653. Next-door Cañon City was once home to the Colorado chapter of the Ku Klux Klan, and several prison administrators told me that their black employees complained about being profiled by the local police.

Beeville is not the heart of heterogeneity either, but it has a bit more racial diversity than Florence because it has a large Hispanic population. Beeville is only 3 percent black, but Hispanics make up almost 68 percent of the population. Beeville has a serious racial divide, with Hispanic and white neighborhoods standing on opposite sides of the railroad tracks. The racial tensions are still obvious in the politics of the town despite protestations to the contrary. Ken Chesshir, the mayor of Beeville, told me that, "You have some old timers, like Arnold (Councilman Arnold Medina) who still screams 'racism' at every turn, but for the most part, things seem to be calmer now. Gilbert Herrera (a young city council member and TDCJ employee) says that we should have a Hispanic mayor, but then Gil has wanted to be mayor since the third day he was on the council."[12]

Chesshir may claim that it is getting better, but Medina abstains from every vote the council takes. Three of the four county commissioners were

Hispanic at the time of my research, but several white local politicians argued that this was because they packed the voting booths, taking busloads of seniors from the local homes to the polls as well as other more unsavory acts. Whether or not this is true or just an urban (or rather rural) myth is up for debate, but it shows the level of distrust between the races in the political world.

Although Beeville has more Hispanics than Florence, both towns' African American populations remain minuscule. In fact, the only blacks I encountered in Beeville were on work crews, and there was something very unnerving in seeing these inmates in their white uniforms, chained together, and doing landscaping and other grunt work. The scene certainly had a slave-like feel to it that made me quite uncomfortable. I often asked about this issue, but none of my interviewees seemed to see the connection as I did. I also asked what the effects might be on a community when the only blacks the residents encountered were incarcerated, but many community members dodged the issue. In fact, most seemed perplexed by the question.[13]

One official did discuss the issue of race with me. He stated that there was a problem in bringing criminally sophisticated urban blacks to Beeville to be watched over by "ignorant country boys" as COs.[14] He claimed that the inmates viewed them as fresh meat and did what they could to corrupt them. He said that they start with small favors, asking COs to mail a letter for them or some such small favor. Such a favor can cost an employee his job, and after one such incident the inmate essentially owns them, threatening to tell a supervisor about the favor unless the officer does more significant ones. Furthermore, the inmates will take advantage when they can. In one such incident, several inmates were indicted for unlawful restraint of a CO. Three inmates held a 19-year-old local CO in a cell during a cell search. Another inmate came out of the cell for the search and after getting on the other side of the CO, claimed that he had to go back in. He then pushed the CO into the cell where the other three grabbed him and held him down. The event ended without injuries, but the incident seems to exemplify the official's concerns.

Despite some differences in these two places, there is much that they share. This is especially true in terms of a similar history in lobbying for a prison facility. This process is an important part of the shared social history of each community and is the most important one in this study. The decision to lobby and the process of lobbying to land a prison changed the face of these two communities, often in ways never imagined. The following section will discuss this significant historical moment and describe the lobbying process in both communities.

SITING AND LOBBYING: THE PRISON DERBY[15]

Overall, the lobbying and siting process is a whirlwind of activity, with community meetings to discuss the proposal to get the prisons and prison officials visiting the towns and holding meetings of their own with community leaders and residents. Communities put together incentive packages to woo the prison away from other contenders and toward their own community. Prison leaders discuss concerns that exist among those few residents who might question the wisdom of bringing a prison into their community, and the entire process reaches a fever pitch. Eventually a decision is made and the real work of opening a prison begins. The following sections describe the lobbying process that took place in each town.

Beeville

According to former city manager and current head of the Bee Economic Development Authority (BEDA) Joe Montez, a Request for Proposals from the Texas Department of Corrections (TDC) ended up on his desk and he began putting out feelers in the community. Montez has been a fixture in South Texas politics for over two decades, moving on to be city manager of Corpus Christi before coming back to Beeville. The TDC (now the Texas Department of Criminal Justice, or TDCJ) made it very clear that they would not consider any sites with significant community opposition.

Historically, prisons were not usually considered a paved road to economic revitalization. Lawsuits and other means of stopping various entities from locating prisons where they had not been before were commonplace.[16] Montez said that he was aware of this and wanted to garner as much support from community leaders as possible before bringing the proposal to the general public. His first move was to enlist the help of Grady Hogue, the highly respected former president of Bee County Community College, to set up the BEDA and to help garner support from Beeville's business and political leaders.

According to Theresa Holland, the executive director of the Beeville Chamber of Commerce, it was her organization that started things. She said, "I know Joe likes to take credit for it, but the whole idea started in this office. We started a petition and when we got the signatures, we started the ball rolling." Whether the proposal started in city hall or at the chamber of commerce, business leaders were open to the idea. The local elected officials took a bit longer to get on board. Montez told me, "I remember the look on the mayor's face when I told him. I said 'We're going to get a prison' and he said 'Are you crazy?'"

Montez decided to go to the Bee County Commissioner's Court instead.[17] The county commissioners were more open to the idea than the city government had been (especially after the petition was completed) and they brought the City Council around. Eventually, the City Council and County Commissioner's Court gave a joint endorsement for the proposal to the TDC.

South Texas politics is a Democrat's game (although Democrat in Texas means something very different than Democrat in the rest of the country), but the tide in the whole state was already turning toward the Republicans. Political savvy led Montez and Hogue to enlist the help of an unlikely ally, Republican County Commissioner Susan Stasny. Stasny is an imposing presence: a tall, blonde former cheerleader from the University of Houston. She is fond of pointing out that she's the only current county commissioner with a college education and has been the only Republican in the county who has managed to stay in office for more than a single term.

"I think they just figured that I knew how to 'talk Republican,' and given the makeup of the committee in charge, they needed someone who could speak the language up in Austin."

The support was there, and Beeville put together a proposal for a maximum-security prison, a so-called 2250, which is a prototypical Texas Prison Unit.[18] Local editorials sang the praises of the proposed prison that would bring in 766 employees and a payroll of $1.3 million a month.[19] In an editorial under the headline "Let's Get Behind Bars," the *Bee Picayune*'s editor, Jeff Latcham, discussed the positive impact of Naval Air Station–Chase Field (this was before it was targeted for closing) and Bee County College as positive trends in the town's development.[20] He stated, "[W]e would encourage citizens to continue the trend of positive, progressive growth by supporting the city's and county's efforts to submit a proposal for a Texas Department of Corrections maximum-security unit here."[21] The article argued that "TDC's job requirements for such a facility is 766 employees resulting in a daily payroll of $43,000-plus ($1.3 million a month)."[22] In addition to discussing the numbers, the editorial asserted that some of the economic advantages also would include:

- It was a clean and stable industry.
- It would help pay off the water district bonds through the sale of the surplus water.
- It would not create a burden on sewer capacity.
- It would create a market for the available housing.[23]

The paper went further, saying, "[l]etters of endorsement from individuals, businesses and organizations are needed." The editorial summed up by saying, "It's important for the community's future. It's important for your future."[24]

Latcham got on his bully pulpit again just five weeks later in an editorial headlined, "Prison Could Salvage our 'Reeling' Economy."[25] The headline was a pun referring to the closing of the Plaza Theatre, which, according to the newspaper, was a sign of the community's tough economic times, and the editorial used the movie *The Last Picture Show* as a metaphor for the town's potential demise. The article focused not only the economic advantages, but also on the classic NIMBY concerns. A chamber of commerce luncheon had been held at which concerns about the prison were discussed and questions were answered by two top TDC officials. Latcham wrote that some of the answers should be comforting to those who envision the classic Hollywood version of a prison town. For instance,

- It is extremely difficult to receive a furlough in the TDC. The only way Beeville would receive furloughed inmates would be if they were headed here anyway.
- No evidence exists that prisoners' families move to the community in which their inmate is incarcerated.
- Prisoners would not be released in Beeville.
- TDC's progressive programs had drastically reduced prison violence and escapes in the past five years.[26]

Latcham then dropped the boom: "It is important for Beeville to pursue this prison, particularly since no other industry is presently knocking at our door."[27] He summed up using his *The Last Picture Show* analogy: "It's important for us to move forward. We'll no doubt see another movie theatre in time, but we certainly can't take that or anything else for granted. Let's make sure that the Plaza was not our last picture show."[28] The push for support worked, and in May 1989, a final version of the proposal to bring the prison to Beeville was prepared and presented to the state legislature.

Bee County made the TDC's first cut and put together a full incentive package. Taken together, the proposal was worth $4.4 million, including $250,000 in cash.[29] This included buying the land; providing water, sewer, and other utilities; and building a new highway bypass. The local chamber of commerce printed up posters and bumper stickers with the slogan "Bee for the Max," with prison bars inside of the letters. Forty-six other Texas communities were also vying for one of the new units.

A short but very politically charged lobbying process ensued with Joe Montez and Grady Hogue pulling every string that they could. On the day of the final decision, several busloads of people went to Austin, posters in hand, to make a last-ditch push. A local college student even dressed up in a bee costume for the event. The Beeville proposal was accepted. In fact, it was the only proposal accepted unanimously by the TDC. What was to become known as the McConnell Unit, named for the former Beeville chief of police, was a reality and opened its gates in 1991.

However, all was not perfect. A few months after the prison siting derby, the town found out that the federal government had decided to close Naval Air Station–Chase Field, the largest employer in the county with 2,100 civilian workers. So what was supposed to be a chance to diversify their economy had become the way to save it. But the closing of the naval base opened up an opportunity for the TDCJ. When a military base closes, the land is first offered to other federal agencies and then to the state. No federal agencies wanted an old military base in Beeville, Texas, so the TDCJ stepped in and took the land. They built two medium-security prison units on this land that serve as the classification units for the TDCJ and built a CO training facility there. The land also houses the regional offices for the TDCJ. The town that had lobbied specifically for a maximum-security unit now also had two medium-security units housing over 5,000 inmates as well as a small minimum-security camp.

Florence

Florence watched its neighboring town of Cañon City gain five new state correctional facilities during the 1980s while its own economy flagged along with the decline of the mining industry. The relationship between the state Department of Corrections (DOC) and Cañon City had been mutually beneficial and Florence was hoping that its relationship with the Federal BOP would be just as positive. Even more so, they hoped that the economic payoffs would be greater. A federal CO's starting salary at the time was around $28,000,[30] far higher than the state's $21,000.[31] During the bidding process, the site coordinator for the BOP, Pat Sledge, said that up to 270 of the 450 positions at the new penitentiary would go to local citizens, a significant number in a town with a population of just over 3,000.[32]

Florence got into the bidding process in May 1987 after Cañon City brought in the BOP to look at 220 acres of land on the outskirts of town that the Benedictine monks had put up for sale. Although the abbey decided to take the property off of the market, the federal government still showed interest in coming to Fremont County. Senator Harold McCormick tried to get the entire state behind the idea of bringing the proposed prison to Colorado, but the legislature killed the measure.

However, Florence went on undaunted. The BOP was hinting that there might be as many as three prisons in the complex (it turned out to be four), and in June 1988, the Florence community went on the offensive, starting a campaign to raise $100,000 to buy a parcel of land on the outskirts of town to donate it to the federal government. In Florence, the head of the local chamber of commerce, Darryl Lindsay, with Fremont Economic Development Corporation head, Skip Dyer, and Florence mayor, Tom McCormick, led the charge.[33] Unlike Beeville, the town did not have the capital to buy the land, so these men went about raising the money from private sources.

The *Cañon City Daily Record* held a poll early in 1988 and 98.2 percent of respondents supported at least some form of a federal prison in Florence. The original proposition was for one 700-bed medium-security prison, one 200-bed minimum-security prison, and the potential for a second medium-security facility with 700 beds and an expansion of 400 beds in the minimum camp. According to the survey, the prison complex would provide 500 jobs and approximately $25 million annually in "local salaries and purchases."[34]

Florence set out to raise the money needed to buy the land to donate it to the federal government. They took individual donations, had a competition between local businesses, held a carnival, and polished the whole thing off with a 24-hour radiothon on June 30, 1988. All told, the town raised more than $126,000. The BOP was impressed by the local show of support, began serious consideration of the town, and performed an environmental impact statement later in the year.

The impact statement was made public in January 1989, and the town held a series of public forums on the proposed prisons in March. The environmental study found no factors that would preclude Fremont County as a potential site and, according to newspaper reports and people who attended the meetings, there were no negative comments made at any of the forums.[35] The BOP then proposed adding a 500-bed maximum-security facility to the project.

Although there were several delays in the actual decision process, Florence was chosen as the site for the new project on October 31, 1989, with construction to be started in the spring of 1990. On December 1, the BOP made an announcement that it would purchase the 400 acres of land itself so that the town could use the money it raised to extend utility lines to the remote location. They also announced that they intended to build another facility on the campus and that this fourth prison would take the place of their Marion facility as the only level-six security prison in the federal system.[36] Level six is the so-called super-max level where the BOP sends the "worst of the worst." Eventually this facility would house such prison superstars as Ramsey Yussef, John Gotti, Ted Kaczynski, and both Oklahoma City bombers. The Administrative Maximum-Security Prison, or ADX, would be a 23-hour-a-day lockdown facility built almost entirely underground.

In December 1989, the Federal BOP opened up an office in downtown Florence. Locals were so desperate for the promised jobs that the headline of the local paper on January 8, 1990, stated "Federal Bureau of Prisons: Don't Apply For Jobs Yet." According to the local BOP office, they had already received numerous calls and letters asking about potential employment, but the BOP stated that it would be at least another year before the hiring process for the promised jobs began.

The groundbreaking on the $150 million project began on July 14 of that year. The project was to be the largest prison complex in the federal system to date. The construction contract went to a contractor from Greeley, Colorado. The Colorado Rural Revitalization Program set up shop. The town braced for the upcoming boom of business on Main Street. According to one newspaper report, construction may have swelled the population of Florence, but construction jobs were not going to locals. Despite this, local residents were preparing for the prison's opening, volunteering for cleanup projects that included plans to reopen the Rialto Theater on Main Street (to date, it is still closed).

The minimum- and medium-security prisons opened their gates, and the first inmates arrived in early 1992. All of the prisons were up and running by December 1994. The prison inmates were sent into the community on various projects, including painting a local school and helping out at a veteran's nursing home. Early reports on the relationship between the town and the prison complex were mostly positive. As one reporter put it, "if one ignores the razor wire around the medium-security prison, the two prisons visible from Colorado 67 look like a campus with mauve and powder-blue buildings."[37]

CONCLUSIONS

What we see above are two very similar stories of an economic development plan that has become more commonplace in the last 20 years. Two rural towns, desperate for jobs and some semblance of industry, turn toward the government to save them from economic ruin. Both towns had a blueprint for this idea. Beeville had long been kept afloat by the military, even when oil and ranching were no longer viable options. Florence had seen its neighbor of Cañon City "thrive" to some extent by depending on the Colorado DOC. It is not surprising, then, that given the opportunity to look for help from a governmental entity, both took advantage of the situation.

Additionally, the time periods are nearly identical. The United States was already in the midst of a changing economy, from the more industrial past to a service-oriented economy. Both towns, lacking in major transportation access or a particularly well-educated and trained populace, had little chance to take advantage of these opportunities. The "dot com" revolution would take place in Texas three hours to the north, in Austin, with its access to the University of Texas. Denver is a boomtown of the West, but is also three hours from the rural community of Florence. Given these circumstances, it hardly seems strange that the local elites got creative and looked to the government to solve their economic crisis.

Neither town may have realized it at the time, but both would become prison hubs housing over 3,000 inmates. Also, the towns put together proposals that just a decade before would have seemed ludicrous. In the early 1980s, states were still imposing their will on communities to find sites for their new facilities and often giving incentives to do so. Of course, prison building in 1980 was a much rarer event than it was in 1988 and 1989, and the changing economic realities made prisons a more feasible if not fully palatable option.

It is difficult to gather what the economic effects have been on these two towns. Several scholars have pointed out the difficulty in measuring the economic effects of local development projects, especially when there have been other intervening factors, as there have been in Beeville and Florence.[38] The raw numbers seem to show that Florence has benefited more, but this is difficult to say with any certainty. What is discernable is what other socioeconomic factors (e.g., race) play a role in this study. The following chapter will argue that social makeup of the towns have a definite effect on the relationship that develops between prison and community.

Despite the differences in socioeconomic factors, the lobbying process was remarkably similar in both communities. What we see is the distinctive shift from a world where prisons are NIMBYs to a world where small rural towns look for an odd form of state economic welfare to insure their continued existence. The prison derby, in which small towns lobby hard for prisons, has taken place in states across the country. This is not to say that all small towns make this choice. The point is that prisons no longer have to use government resources to convince a locality to allow them to bring in a facility. State departments of corrections and the BOP can sit back and choose between competing offers from rural towns. Offers of land, improved septic and water systems, roads, and straight-up cash payments are now the norm. This would not be a problem if it did not lead to expectations that the prisons cannot always meet, be it shopping at local stores or employing significant numbers of local residents.

The main difference between the two towns is in who was being lobbied for a facility. Florence was specifically interested in a federal prison, whereas Beeville was lobbying the state. This, more than anything else, is the most divergent issue between the two towns. The difference between the relationships Beeville would have with the TDCJ and Florence's relationship with the BOP were not a consideration at the time of the lobbying process and would not become evident for several years. It is this difference, more than any other, that will be analyzed in the rest of this book.

NOTES

1. Greenhouse et al., *Law and Community in Three American Towns*, 10.
2. *Ibid.,* 11.

3. *Ibid.*, 158–161.

4. *Ibid.*, 12.

5. *Ibid.*, 149.

6. Guerra, "State Has Helped Beeville Develop a 'Working-Poor' Economy."

7. Redding, *Methland: Death and Life of an American Small Town*.

8. For the BOP's general rules about contacts with vendors, see http://www.bop.gov/business/how.jsp. The full BOP regulations can be found at http://www.bop.gov/policy/progstat/4100_004.pdf. This is a 133-page document that describes in detail what the BOP requires for a business to become a vendor.

9. Hooks et al., "The Prison Industry: Carceral Expansion and Employment in U.S. Counties, 1969–1994." McShane et al., "Prison Impact Studies: Some Comments on Methodological Rigor."

10. All of the data cited in this section were retrieved from http://factfinder.census.gov/home/saff/main.html?_lang=en.

11. As one black warden told me, "I can't even find anyone here who can give me a haircut," personal communication, August 2003.

12. Personal communication, February 2004.

13. Several colleagues and I are currently working on a survey study to see if there is more implicit and explicit racism in prison towns as compared with other rural areas.

14. Personal communication, March 2004.

15. These histories are compiled mainly from interviews, but also from the two local newspapers—*The Bee-Picayune* and *The Cañon City Daily Record*—and two local history books—Margaret Moser's wonderfully detailed *The Biography of a Particular Place* (2001) about Bee County and Rosemae Campbell's *From Trappers to Tourists* (1972) about Fremont County, Colorado. Moser, *The Biography of a Particular Place: Bee County from the Days of the Spanish Missions through September 11, 2001*. Campbell, *From Trappers to Tourists: Fremont County, 1830–1950*.

16. Carlson, "Doing Good and Looking Bad: A Case Study of Prison/Community Relations."

17. Texas seems to have an obsession with naming entities differently than the rest of the country. Prisons are "units" and the county government is the "commissioner's court," with the county judge as the head. The county judge is not a judge in the usual sense of the word, but the political leader of the county.

18. A 2,250-unit actually holds 2,900 inmates when the Trusty Camp is added to the population.

19. Latcham, "Let's Get Behind Bars," *Bee Picayune*, February 20, 1989, p. A4.

20. Note that all of these are governmental or quasi-government developments, not industrial ones.

21. Latcham, "Let's Get Behind Bars," *Bee Picayune*, February 20, 1989, p. A4.

22. *Ibid*. The number of jobs that would go to locals as opposed to those who would be transferred in wasn't discussed in great detail at any point during the siting process.

23. Latcham, 1989b, p. A4

24. *Ibid*.

25. *Ibid*.

26. *Ibid*.

27. *Ibid*.

28. *Ibid*.

29. The actual proposal was given to the author by Beeville City Manager Ford Patton.

30. http://www.bop.gov/hrmpg/hrmcorrectionalofficer.html.

31. http://www.gssa.state.co.us/announce/job+announcements.nsf/5a50 e7ae62411f9e872564db004c6ce2/62d2067e2be56adf87256e51007bfff4?OpenD ocument.

32. *Cañon City Record*, January 25, 1989.

33. Unfortunately, Skip Dyer and Tom McCormick have passed away, so I only have Darryl Lindsay's recollection, in addition to newspaper reports, to go on.

34. The fact that the number of jobs proposed keeps changing is not due to poor research on my part. The proposed number of prisons and types of prisons kept changing until the final number of four was reached. As the proposal changed, so did the number of purported jobs that would go to the local community, although all estimates were based on an assumption that 60 percent of jobs would go to locals.

35. *Florence Citizen*, March 30, 1989.

36. Alcatraz was the first level-six facility in the federal system, but it was replaced by Marion when it closed in 1963.

37. *Cañon City Record*, January 25, 1989.

38. Feicock, "The Effects of Economic Development Policy of Local Economic Growth."

Chapter Four

Citizens and Hermits

We don't have enough water to bring in a brewery and IBM ain't exactly knocking on the door. What the hell else were we supposed to do?
Benny Johnson, Former Mayor of Cañon City, Colorado

One becomes aware fairly quickly that Beeville is a prison town. Whether it is the occasional group of inmates in their stark white jumpsuits doing the landscaping at the county courthouse or the very common sight of a uniformed corrections officer (CO) at the H-E-B, there is little doubt that there is a prison nearby. This is not the case in Florence. You could easily spend a week in town and not see any sign of the federal facilities on the outskirts of town. In fact, signs of the East Cañon Prison complex, run by the Colorado Department of Corrections (CDOC) in the neighboring town, are far more common. One could even drive by the prison complex itself without being able to tell that over 3,000 inmates lived there because the more secure facilities cannot be seen from the highway.

As the relationships between the prison and the community developed in Beeville and Florence, one overarching issue became obvious—the difference in the relationships between the prisons and the communities in each town. In Florence, the federal government, through the Bureau of Prisons (BOP), remains in the background. Of course, everyone in town knows that the prisons are there, but even in comparison to next-door Cañon City, they do not stick out. Cañon City seems to revolve around the prisons. In fact, the "Old Max" territorial prison, opened in 1871, is right downtown. The same cannot be said of next-door Florence.

Unlike Cañon City, Beeville does not have over 100 years as a prison town, but it does seem to be just as dominated by its major industry. The state (in this case, the Texas Department of Criminal Justice, or TDCJ) and the community are deeply linked. This difference, state or federal prisons, is an important part of the story. From the prison's side, this is a story about federalism and political responsiveness. This story is told in various forms by all three institutions discussed in this book. The difference between the state and the federal government tells only part of the story. When it comes to the prisons and community relations, individual wardens matter. Therefore the competing story from the prison's side is actually two tales: the overarching tale of the difference between the federal prisons and the state prisons in these two towns and the tale of the effectiveness of individual wardens.

Wardens have become more political and less autonomous figures over the past 30 years, but despite this, they are still very powerful figures. An individual warden works within the bureaucracy of his department of corrections but has a large role to play in the relationship with the community. I argue that there are two types of wardens: "the citizen" and "the hermit."

This chapter focuses on the relationship between the community and prison from the standpoint of the prison. It begins by outlining some of the differences between the natures of federal and state bureaucracies and links that to the differences between state-run prison institutions and federal prisons, specifically in Texas and Colorado. It discusses the changes in prison management over time and the increasing politicization of prison management. It then describes the problems faced by wardens in their relationship with the community and discusses the difference between citizens and hermits in more detail. It concludes with a section on prison work crews sent into the community by wardens to do various service projects as an example of one tool in a warden's toolbox to foster community relations. In my cases, the use of the work crews was one measure through which the difference between citizens and hermits could be seen.

POLITICAL RESPONSIVENESS

Although most people would not consider prisons political entities, spending on corrections has made this proposition hard to take seriously. For example, Texas spent nearly $3 billion on its corrections department, nearly 7 percent of its total general fund budget.[1] Prisons have become politicized and as such are subject to political pressures.

The state prisons, the entities closer to "the people," appeared to be more responsive to community concerns and more concerned with their image in the community. I argue that there are three reasons for this. The first has to do with electoral concerns and constituency size. A state legislator is going to be much more concerned with her small district and its concerns than a member of Congress. The second reason has to do with the nature of bureaucracy, in which bigger is not necessarily better when it comes to the responsiveness of the government to the citizenry. The third reason has to do with the attitude of the employees toward the residents of the community. In the two towns in this study, state employees were far more engaged in the community around them than the federal employees.

The Federal BOP has over 180 prisons, with facilities in 38 states plus one in Puerto Rico. The Attorney General appoints its director and the BOP is under the auspices of the Department of Justice. The TDCJ is responsible for almost 100 facilities and has prisons in nearly every county in Texas. It is overseen by the Texas Board of Criminal Justice, which is composed of nine members who are appointed by the governor for staggered six-year terms. It is easy to see that the geographic reach of the BOP is significantly larger than that of the TDCJ, but they also have more bureaucratic insulation from their constituency than their Texas counterpart.

Scholars have often argued that in the policy arena, states are more innovative than the federal government and may indeed be, to paraphrase Justice Brandeis, "laboratories for democracy."[2] But the question of whether or not they are more responsive to the citizenry is questionable, despite some literature on the topic.[3] However, in this study, the administrative agency of the state appeared to be much more responsive to local concerns than its federal counterpart.

Why does this appear to be so? The first reason may have to do with electoral concerns and constituency size. State elected officials are generally more accessible as compared with federal officials, and state representatives are going to be much more responsive to a constituent's concerns than their counterpart in the U.S. House of Representatives. Even a small town is important to a state representative when election time comes around. This will not necessarily be so with members of the U.S. House of Representatives. In fact, a state legislature needs the votes of a small rural community much more than a member of Congress. For example, in Beeville, the 12,000 residents make up over 11 percent of their state representative's electoral base. This means that the state representative must be responsive to community concerns to get elected. However, Florence's 4,000 residents make up less than 0.5 percent of the electoral base for their member of the U.S. House of Representatives. A member of the House can all but ignore such a small part of his constituency. This is not to say that members of Congress are unresponsive to small towns, but it will be much more likely that local concerns will be heard at the state level than at the federal level.

Not only are state elected officials more likely to respond to their constituencies than federal ones, the bureaucratic agencies here are also of a vastly different scale. To understand just how different, consider that in 2006, the TDCJ had an operating budget of just over $2.5 billion, whereas the Department of Justice, of which the BOP is one part, has a $22 billion-plus total budget. The BOP also has nearly twice as many employees as the TDCJ.[4] A larger bureaucratic agency is less likely to be concerned with a small rural community and its problems. It is also much more difficult to respond to local concerns from Washington.

The final reason may come down to what I can only term "the sophistication" of the employees of the federal government. In my observations, prison employees, especially the upper management, stood out from the average person in Fremont County. According to several studies, prison workers can be cliquish as a rule and do not tend to socialize with people outside of the fold.[5] Even so, this is more profound among federal employees. Part of the problem is that many employees choose to live elsewhere, usually the larger cities within commuting distance. But local citizens seem to feel that they are treated with disdain by the employees at the federal prison, a complaint that I did not hear in reference to state employees. Federal employees remain outsiders in the communities in which they serve.

TDCJ VERSUS. BOP: IT'S ALL ABOUT THE DISTANCE

In other ways, the TDCJ's Division of Institutions and the Federal BOP are quite similar. As of June 22, 2006, BOP-run facilities were home to 161,719 inmates.[6] As of August 31, 2005, 152,213 inmates were being held in TDCJ-run facilities.[7] At the end of fiscal year 2004, the BOP had 35,023 employees involved with security, whereas the TDCJ had a security staff of 26,926.[8] In many statistical ways, they are ideally situated for comparison. So there is a question as to how two seemingly similar institutions can interact so differently with their host towns. The answer may lie in the difference between state and federal institutions as a whole.

The former Director of Institutions for the TDCJ, Doug Dretke, argued that a large part of this had to do with the difference in the physical and bureaucratic distance between a state and federal entity. "In my capacity, I would get calls from State Legislators who got complaints from constituents." He would then filter those complaints down to the institutions. He speculated that federal prison wardens may never hear about such complaints. Robert Treon, former director of Region IV for the TDCJ, seconded this proposition but added that in his capacity, he often had to walk a tightrope between the local government and state legislature, who often have very different priorities. No BOP employees mentioned having to do this same dance.

There are institutional factors that make it easier for state prison managers to be more responsive to community concerns. First and foremost is the length of tenure of upper management in Texas as opposed to the BOP. One warden told me that even when there are good relations between a warden and the community for the BOP, these wardens are moved out so quickly that the relationship never has time to flourish.[9] Although a warden who wants to get ahead in the TDCJ may want to get to Huntsville, because this is where the home office is as well as eight TDCJ units, one can have a long career while remaining in the hinterlands like Beeville. And by remaining in the hinterlands for longer, a state prison employee is much more likely to become an insider in the community in which they serve.

Time and again I heard how involved former warden Thomas Prasifka and former Region IV director Doug Dretke were in the community in Beeville. Prasifka, now a deputy director of the Institutions Division in Huntsville, told me that he considered being a part of the community as an element of his job once he rose above the rank of major (the highest uniformed rank in the department). Prasifka said that a large part of his involvement was because he had kids in school, and although he kept stressing this point, I felt that his involvement seemed to go beyond just being a father.

Prasifka also instilled the importance of this to his employees. He argued that his former warden, Wayne Scott, had discussed this with him and he felt that he needed to pass it on. One of his former majors, Danny Fernandez, understood this. Fernandez is a local Beeville kid who has moved up the ranks from a CO, the highest-ranking local in Beeville. He told me that Prasifka was adamant that Fernandez understood his role, not only as a major on the unit, but also as a "hometown boy made good." He is TDCJ's best PR for locals to come and work there because one of their own, a consummate "insider," has moved up the ranks. Fernandez is a fixture in the Hispanic and white communities in Beeville, appearing at the local high school on behalf of the TDCJ as well as at local events.

The fact that Fernandez has stayed in Beeville while still being promoted is evidence of how the TDCJ views community relations. Fernandez has worked in all three units in Beeville at various times, changing from one to another with each promotion. Although former director Dretke said that Fernandez may need to be moved to progress further in his career, the decision to keep him in Beeville for as long as possible was made, in part, with the community in mind. Locals, Dretke argued, especially Hispanics, need to see that there are opportunities within the TDCJ for a long and successful career. Fernandez is walking proof of this.

Having community insiders who work at the facility adds to the responsiveness by the facility to community concerns. Having a major who grew up there or local politicians who work at the prison, something we see in Beeville, can mean that issues are directly discussed with the prison administration and never have to go through the system.

As discussed in chapter three, insider status is an important one in notions of community, and studies have long found a dichotomy between the insider and the outsider as being a troubling one, especially in economic development projects. In Beeville and Florence, the insider/outsider distinction certainly exists, but in a form that is more obvious and more complex than in other places. The opening of a prison requires a large influx of experienced personnel. This group of newcomers becomes the "other"—the boogeyman whom insiders can blame for the breakdown of their community. These new people often feel that they are held up to a different standard, that all of their mistakes are multiplied because they work at the prison.[10]

This is not to say that the employees have not brought some of these problems on themselves. Many local citizens, when asked if the prisons have brought problems to the community, respond that the COs are the ones who have proven to be problematic, not inmates or their families, a concern often cited by older "not in my back yard" (NIMBY)-related studies of the issue. Often prison officials were not only aware of the problems with their employees, they were quite open about them. For example, one of the consistent complaints by Beeville residents was that

TDCJ employees wrote "hot checks," in which one writes a check despite having insufficient funds in the account. When I asked the regional director what he thought the biggest problem was between employees and the community, and he admitted that it was COs writing hot checks. The director understood that some new employees were just kids getting their first sizable paycheck and that in the process, they often get in over their heads financially by buying new cars and other items on credit and then writing checks that will bounce to pay for those items.

The BOP has much more stringent hiring practices, as will be discussed in chapter five, which include a credit report, so I did not hear complaints about hot checks in Florence, but in both communities, issues surrounding family violence were often mentioned. Several studies have been done showing increased rates of family violence on military bases,[11] but I have also found anecdotal evidence that this is prevalent among COs. In fact, several prison administrators were very open about this problem, with one telling me "we teach them how to deal with the inmates at work, but we don't teach them how to deal with their families when they get home."

It is issues such as this that keeps the prison employees as outsiders to the old guard in the community. Even in Beeville, where many of the prison jobs go to locals and the TDCJ has made itself more a part of the community, those who "wear the gray" (a reference to the colors of the TDCJ uniforms) are still outsiders to a certain extent. It is in just this way that locals discuss the criminal and family problems among the prison employees. However, these state employees are much more readily accepted than their federal counterparts. TDCJ employees become involved in the local community, and the TDCJ itself seems to work harder to make sure this is so. There also seem to be several institutional and bureaucratic factors that have an influence. Overall, the state of Texas is generally in a better position to foster good community relations, but there is more to the story than this. Individual wardens have a part to play. However, before discussing these individual wardens, I will first discuss how the job of warden and prison managers more generally has changed over time.

CHANGES IN PRISON MANAGEMENT

Prison policy may be set in Washington, D.C., or state capitols, but what actually happens inside of the razor wire is heavily influenced by the man or woman at the top. Even so, wardens do not have the same level of autonomy as in the past. The era of the "big boss warden" is gone and the rise of the bureaucratic prison has taken hold, but this does not mean that the warden does not, in many ways, have his own fiefdom inside of the prison walls.[12] This section discusses the professionalization and bureaucratization of prison administration while outlining the continued importance of the individual warden to an institution and in matters of community relations.

Bureaucratization of the prison system has attempted to standardize prison policy over different institutions within the same department. The prison-building boom has been, at least in part, the reason for this.[13] In the past, many states had only one or just a handful of prisons of the same security level, which were easy to oversee. The building boom has necessitated a certain amount of consistency across many institutions and bureaucratization of the system as a whole.[14]

For example, the TDCJ has a 101-page handbook for offenders explaining the rules for everything from rights to showers, to eligibility for parole, to prisoner litigation procedures.[15] There is a separate handbook that describes just disciplinary rules and procedures.[16] Such bureaucratic measures are meant to make the system more uniform, but even with these, this is not always the case. Despite this attempt at uniformity, different wardens and prison administrators selectively enforce rules and regulations, and despite the corrections communities' attempts to make things more consistent, what goes on inside of the prison is still, in large part, up to those running the individual institutions.[17]

In part because of this bureaucratization, interest in prison management has grown, although it is not nearly as widely studied as it might be. John DiIulio's work, nearly 20 years old now and done before the prison-building boom really took its full effect, was the first time that prison administration was front and center in the prison scholarship. DiIulio's main focus moved away from inmate-centered studies and tried to give an alternative to what he deems the "sociological view of prisons."[18] Although several other scholars began this interest in the changing role of prison administrator,[19] it is DiIulio who really delves into the subject, arguing that it is prison management (not other issues such as overcrowding and inmate behavior) that really matters in the effective running of a prison.

Although some may question his conclusions,[20] DiIulio's work led to a greater interest in prison managers, and as a result, academics began to challenge many of the sociological assumptions about prison life.[21] As assumptions were changing, so was the profession of prison managers. Thirty years ago, most states had no more than a few large maximum-security prisons to house all of their inmates. This is no longer the case. More enlightened and more complicated classification systems have led to the building of medium- and minimum-security institutions in addition to the maximum-security facilities. There are also specialized facilities for sex offenders, mentally ill inmates, and gang members. This change, coupled with the inmate population boom, led to the aforementioned prison-building boom. More prisons meant more prison managers, and these managers were better educated and more bureaucratically and politically savvy than their predecessors.

The change from the prison as fiefdom to a more bureaucratized entity has been well documented,[22] and correctional administrators are now likely to have BA and MA degrees hanging prominently on their walls.[23] They move from institution to institution much more often than in the past, and increased levels of bureaucracy have led to promotion opportunities above the rank of senior warden. With these changes, prison executives have become more involved in the world outside of the fences. According to Kevin Wright, modern prison executives spend 70 percent of their time dealing with issues outside of the prison walls.[24] This has forced prison administrators to become much more public relations oriented than ever before.

According to Wright, there are two major factors that have led to this. First, is the added involvement of the courts in the day-to-day running of a prison.[25] A major part of a warden's job was about keeping incidents minor enough so that they did not make the papers, but now a warden has to deal with meeting accreditation standards, court cases, court orders, and the abundance of politicians coming into their institutions. Prisons are still closed societies to a great extent, but they are far more open than were in the past, and the proliferation of inmate lawsuits has definitely played a part in this.

The second and probably more important reason for this shift is purely a question of numbers.[26] More inmates serving longer sentences means that corrections budgets are a far larger part of a state's overall expenditures. The politicization of crime and prisons has been well documented, and with this increased attention, prison executives have become increasingly involved in policy matters. As Wright puts it, "Clearly, modern prison system executives must be astute political creatures. They must have an understanding of the political process along with a willingness and an ability to participate as never before."[27] The modern prison executive is getting to be far more like an executive of a major corporation than a "keeper of the keys." They have to be familiar with concepts such as total quality management and cost-benefit analyses. This is not to say that custody and control have ceased to be the primary concern of prison officials. It is just that there are other functions that have become more and more important with time.

The greater interest from politicians has also added to the public interest. As Wright notes, the proliferation of news sources and tenacity of many journalists have added to the increased public interest, and senior prison officials are expected to deal with the media far more than ever before.[28] More importantly, perhaps, is that the increased public awareness of crime has led to increased awareness of prisons themselves. Beyond just morbid fascination with the major incidents, taxpayers believe they have a right to know how their money is being spent.

More money spent on prisons also means more money spent to study them, leading to a sort of prison academic-industrial complex. Sykes and Jacobs's works were groundbreaking in their times, in part because they went somewhere no one had gone before, but nowadays the sight of a sociologist in a prison is not particularly rare. In fact, many departments of corrections have their own research offices that conduct internal studies and deal with outside academics who wish to study the institutions. Although the focus of most of these studies is still inmate-centered, there are few aspects of prison life that have not been or are not currently being studied. When I asked a local prosecutor why he thought I was able to gain access to the prisons without too much difficulty, he said that the prison system was "so used to having people traipsing around the grounds, why would one more idiot asking questions bother them?"[29]

THE POLITICS OF PRISON MANAGEMENT

Although some scholars have begun to see the added importance of external relations to prison administrators, they do not look at the importance of those relations on the local level.[30] Most of the discussion centers on relationships with state- and federal-level political actors while ignoring those actors closest to the institutions themselves. According to Wright, it is in the relationship with state- and federal-level actors where the prison administrator as public relations director is at its core.[31] However, this ignores that the public relations part of the warden's job also means dealing with the local government and community. Prison executives may have to learn to walk the hallways of the legislature as well as they walk the tiers of their prisons, but they need to walk down Main Street as well. In other words, prison administrators not only need to foster relations with state politicians, they need to do so with local politicians in the town in which they are located.

Even if policies inside of a facility are more uniform than in the past, a warden's relationship with the outside community has not seen as much change because there is little guidance from the home office as to how the senior staff must act. The handbooks and court orders may regulate what goes on inside of an institution, but how the warden and senior staff deal with the local community and government is, to a large extent, up to each individual warden.

This is not to say that the home office has no say in the matter. For example, the BOP has community-relations boards in most communities that house a prison that meet quarterly. This board is made up of local politicians, business leaders, and law enforcement who meet with senior staff to get a better understanding of what goes on inside of the institution. These meetings are meant to be a forum for the open exchange of concerns but more often are just a forum for surface presentations by the prison administrators about inmate programs. A warden's personal relationships, especially in rural communities, matter much more. Some departments of corrections realize this and try to instill the importance of community relations to their senior staff. The former Director of Institutions for the TDCJ told me that this was something he discussed with every new senior warden.[32] Whether or not the warden takes the director's advice to heart appears to depend on the individual warden.

CITIZENS AND HERMITS

Thomas Jefferson once wrote to James Madison that a public servant should be constantly at his post.[33] For Jefferson, the highest honor of citizenship was to be given such a post. The warden of a prison is just such a public servant, although not all understand that their post stretches beyond the razor wire of their facility. There are two types of wardens when it comes to this understanding: the citizen and the hermit.[34] Although wardens have the most interaction with the community, their assistants and even some of the highest-ranking uniformed staff have a role to play, and all senior staff fit into this model. They are all representatives of the institutions and are looked to by the members of the community as such.

Like any typology or categorization, this one is not without its problems. The either/or nature of this model simplifies some of these problems, but this does not make it perfect. Some wardens and senior staff will act against type from time to time, but my research has shown a significant consistency in their behavior.[35] Consistency is vital to good prison management and this alone may explain this, but remarkably, even in a crisis, citizens remain citizens and hermits hide out.

The citizen is the most visible in the community. He is a citizen in the strongest Jeffersonian sense of the word in a place that comes closest to being a modern Jeffersonian ward republic, the small rural community. Although I do not share Jefferson's and others' romantic notions about rural America, they are undoubtedly places of intense personal contact and handshake deals. The citizen seems to instinctually understand this. He or she will be active in local civic groups, enthusiastically try to educate the public, and tend to be visible about town. In towns with multiple facilities and an ever-changing administration, many top managers are unknown to the general population. The citizen will not only be known, he will be known by first name. One citizen became so involved that he eventually became mayor after he retired. Other citizens have become city counselors and county commissioners as well as becoming involved in the local community in various other capacities.

There are four major attributes that all citizen wardens share. The first is accessibility. The citizen warden will be available to the community for various events and reachable by the local government, especially in times of stress. The second attribute is openness. All of my interviewees acknowledged that all prisons are bound to have problems at some point. The citizen gives as much information as possible without jeopardizing the safety of employees and inmates. Especially in a small community where rumors run rampant, official word about problems that arise can be very important to the community at large.

Third, the citizen warden is a charismatic figure. In many ways, the role of the warden in community relations is that of an educator. He must teach the public about the truths and myths of life in prison. The citizen warden takes this part of his job very seriously and understands the importance of this function. The final attribute is confidence. The citizen warden is confident in his own abilities and that of his staff. This is especially important when it comes to the use of community-service squads—inmates who go out in the community to perform various functions. The citizen warden will be confident enough in his staff to protect the public from the inmates.

On the other hand, the hermit lacks many or all of these qualities. The hermit warden acts as an administrator first and cares little for public relations. He will not use the tools at his discretion, such as the community-service squads to try to build up goodwill with the town. He avoids public appearances and rarely, if ever, is in contact with local governmental officials. Hermits will send their assistants to community relations board meetings and will be unavailable to the local media. This type of behavior will only hinder relations with the community.

One citizen told me that he thought that having kids in the local schools made a big difference for him. "What kind of parent would I be if I wasn't involved?" he asked.[36] When he reached the rank of major, his warden told him that it was now a part of his job to "meet folks" and be a community representative for the prisons. He took this part of his job very seriously, joining the chamber of commerce, heading up the stock show organizing committee, and attending school board meetings. His son was a star football player at the local high school, and the warden attended all of his games.

The local sheriff told me that many days, he and this warden had coffee and visited for a while.[37] This gave them an opportunity to discuss local issues and problems. The sheriff loaned the warden his people and the warden monitored his police scanner and offered help when there was a large accident on the local highway. The warden was also very generous with his inmates. Community-service squads performed various work around town, including painting the county courthouse and landscaping projects, something discussed in more detail below.

The citizen is concerned with making sure that the relationship with the community as a whole is as strong as possible. Many of the managers who I spoke with said that the public had many misunderstandings about what went on inside of their facilities, but very few actively did anything about it. The citizen will set up tours for local political and business leaders. He makes himself available for the local media, even in times of trouble. On the whole, prisons tend to be very secretive places, and the citizen tries to open them up as best he can without putting security in jeopardy. One citizen put it to me in the following way: he said, "There are times when we screw up and there are times when things get screwed up. We need to educate the public so they can recognize the difference."[38]

The citizen is aware and open about the kinds of problems their employees have. This kind of openness can only help bring problems to the forefront. As is discussed below, not everyone is so open to such discussions. The hermit would prefer to bury issues like domestic violence and other problems with their employees. The hermit hides in his institution and has as little dealings with the community as possible. The hermit sees his job as ending at the walls of his institution and does not see or does not care about the problems of the community. One such warden put it to me this way, "I can sit back and watch what goes on, the fights and the petty political stuff, and I don't want to be involved. I've got enough to deal with in here and it's all I can do to make sure that I get out from behind this desk and walk around every day."[39]

Wardens are inundated with invitations to local events, and the hermit chooses not to attend even when there is time in his schedule. "Sometimes I don't feel like hanging out with my neighbors after I've spent 12 hours at work," one warden told me.[40] But it seems that there is more than tiredness that can affect the relationship. Some wardens told me that they felt like they were treated as outsiders by the community and that their employees were often singled out by local law enforcement and given speeding tickets and other moving violations. Interestingly, community residents often report that they find prison employees cliquish and unfriendly. Either way, a hermit will not help matters.

WORK CREWS

The most glaring difference between citizens and hermits shows itself in the use of work crews or community-service squads—groups of inmates who go into the community to perform community-service projects. In many ways, the use of work crews is one measure that, in my two cases, seems to be the most obvious difference between the citizen and the hermit. According to a report on prison labor by the National Institute of Corrections, "community-service work is not essential to jail or prison operations, its net costs to the facility are higher than those associated with in-house work programs . . . However, benefits to the community may offset the direct costs to the jail or prison and indirectly benefit the facility itself."[41] What is problematic about this conclusion is that the report has no data to back up this claim. However, many prison managers echo this conclusion, and despite the difficulty in measuring this, it appears to be true.

Prison labor has long been an issue for prison managers. Over time, two models of prison labor have developed. The first is prison labor for profit. The notion and use of prison labor for profit inside and outside of a facility has long been a complicated one. The shadow of convict lease programs of the 1800s, in which inmates were leased out to local farms to work essentially as slaves, still looms large. However, in recent years, such programs have become more popular. But prisons have always been hotbeds of idleness, and with the decline of the rehabilitative programs of the 1960s and 1970s, the issue has only worsened. Before the recent advent of private prisons contracting prison labor to private corporations, the lines of what prison laborers could and could not do were fairly clear: They could work for minimal pay as long as the contracts for goods were only for state entities.

The second model of prison labor is labor for the good of the facility itself. As opposed to prison labor for profit ventures, prison labor to promote self-sufficiency has long been used and has rarely caused controversy. The concept of inmates working the fields for food that will be used inside of the prison walls has always been popular with the general public, especially in the prison farms of the South, where it saves an enormous amount of tax dollars. Additionally, inmates have always been used for day-to-day general maintenance duties around the facility, from preparing meals to cleaning the cell blocks.

Community-service squads do not really fit either model of prison labor. Inmates on these squads do not make any marketable product, nor does their work help the prison run in any tangible way. They also seem to fall through the cracks in terms of most current case law because they work outside the prison, but not for a private firm. The courts have not heard an appeal directly on this issue, but there may be a reason for this. Inmates work hard to get on these work crews because it means a rare trip outside of the facility and the chance to break up the boredom that is such a major part of prison life. Sometimes there are added bonuses. One local work crew in Beeville got McDonald's cheeseburgers from the local chamber of commerce after fixing their roof, a treat most prisoners will never get. Only the best-behaved inmates are allowed on these work crews because the risk of escape or some other major problem is so great. That may be why prisoners, normally a very litigious group, have not been nearly as litigious on the issue of community-work squads.[42]

In addition to the problematic chain-gang-like imagery, there is also the fear of escapes. For example, Beeville only lobbied for a maximum-security prison because they wanted as little interaction with the inmates as possible. Most communities learn to appreciate the free work given to them by the prisons, and inmates have been used to clean up after floods; fix up courthouses, cemeteries, and local landmarks; and do various other improvement projects.

The TDCJ leaves it up to the local warden to decide how or even if to use their community-service squads. These squads have been very busy, especially during Warden Thomas Prasifka's reign in the McConnell Unit. His inmates cleaned up a flooded stream in town, fixed the roof of the Chamber of Commerce building, and made sand bags when a hurricane was bearing down on South Texas. Inmates do almost all of the landscaping at the local courthouse and gave the building its recent facelift. The service squads in their white jumpsuits have become commonplace in the town.

Florence's prison inmates have also done work around the town, but the amount seems to have declined over time. The prison still does some small things, like the sign they built for Pioneer Park, the local recreational park, but they do not do as much outside work for the community. When the prisons first opened, there seemed to be more inmates working around the community, participating in cleanup projects in the downtown area and refurbishing the Rialto Theatre. However, such projects have diminished over time, mostly because the town stopped asking for help.

A warden who understands what these services mean to the local community (i.e., the citizen warden) and cares about the working relationship will extensively use the service squads. Inmate workers have been used to clean up after floods, maintain old cemeteries, and fix roofs on public buildings. But as discussed in chapter three, communities will often specifically lobby for a maximum-security institution so that there is as little interaction with the inmate population as possible.[43] The community-service squads ensure that the community will not have this security. So why would communities, such as Beeville, that specifically did not want inmates in their midst so openly welcome these work squads after the prison opened?

The answer may come down to money. In Cañon City, Colorado, Florence's next-door neighbor and home to eight state prison facilities of its own, inmates are used to perform various cleanup tasks around the community, including cleaning up a historic cemetery. Because of budget cutbacks, the CDOC stopped sending out the squads. The city manager of Cañon City estimated that the city now had to pay out over $20,000 to do the projects that the CDOC inmates used to do.[44] This may not seem like a huge amount of money, but to a small town in Colorado, it is significant.

For example, in Beeville, the TDCJ work squads were often cited to me as one of the positives that the prison has brought. The county has recently undertaken a $6.1 million project to renovate the county courthouse to its original 1912 grandeur and expand some offices inside. Inmates have always been used to do the landscaping for the building and were again used on the landscaping during the renovations. Although I found no estimates for how much the county saved, it is surely a significant amount for a poor rural county.

However, beyond the money, the community seems to warm to the idea of these service squads over time. According to several TDCJ administrators, the initial trepidation about inmate work crews is common in new prison towns, but once the public is educated to the benefits of these work crews and convinced of their safety, they welcome the free labor. The ability of the department in convincing the community of this may be about a warden's personal charisma as much as anything else.[45]

Although all departments encourage inmate work crews, it is ultimately up to each individual warden how much they farm out their labor pool. Doug Dretke, former Director of Institutions for the TDCJ, seems to feel that a warden's likelihood to use these squads has to do with a warden's overall confidence level.[46] He said that a confident warden understands the potential risks but trusts himself and his staff to see the benefits that outweigh any potential problems. He is also secure in his own ability to deal with a problem should one come up.

But other than personal appearances by senior staff, the use of the work crew seems to be the most visible and most appreciated tool in the warden's toolbox to warm the relationship with a community. Something as simple as having the prison's wood-making shop make a sign for a local park is greatly appreciated. Outside work crews are even more appreciated, although they take some getting used to for the community's residents.

There may be other ways for a citizen warden to foster good community relations, but the use of work crews is possibly the most visible. However, using these squads can be a difficult proposition, and the individual warden must be confident in his and his staff's abilities to use them regularly. The citizen warden understands their importance and is willing to take the risks; the hermit warden is not. According to one source, this is because the hermit does not trust in his own abilities or those of his staff to do so securely.

CONCLUSIONS

The difference between the relationships a community has with a state prison as opposed to a federal prison may, in fact, have much broader implications beyond just the prison world. As localities become more involved in the economic development world, choices about who to lobby for projects looms large.[47] Additionally, the citizen and hermit typologies discussed here may be applicable beyond just prisons. Even so, these issues have repercussions for all communities with a facility or those interested in lobbying to get one.

The story of how prisons such as those in Beeville and Florence develop relationships with the towns that house them is an important one, but it has not been discussed elsewhere in the prison impact literature. By observing Beeville and Florence, we get a first glimpse of the various factors that give a state prison a better chance than a federal facility to become an institutional member of a community. Despite these difficulties, wardens in both systems can help or hinder the development of this relationship. The following chapter will tell the community's side of the story—a story of expectations and disappointments in terms of the realities that a prison can and cannot deliver.

NOTES

1. http://www.pewcenteronthestates.org/uploadedFiles/wwwpewcen teronthestatesorg/Fact_Sheets/PSPP_1in31_factsheets_FINAL_WEB.pdf, retrieved on June 16, 2009.

2. *New State Ice Co. v. Liebmann*, 285 U.S. 262, at 311 (1932), Brandeis dissenting.

3. Wood et al., *Bureaucratic Dynamics: The Role of Bureaucracy in a Democracy.*

4. This is true although they have nearly identical numbers of employees working in their security forces, those who actually deal directly with inmates. This means that the BOP has a much greater percentage of employees in administrative and bureaucratic duties.

5. Fleischer, *Warehousing Violence.* Wright, "The World of Work Has Changed! So What Does This Mean for Correctional Management?"

6. The BOP updates its prison population statistics weekly at http://www.bop.gov/locations/weekly_report.jsp, retrieved on June 22, 2006. This number does not include those held in private facilities or community corrections-management offices.

7. http://www.tdcj.state.tx.us/publications/executive/FY2005_Statistical_Report.pdf.

8. http://www.bop.gov/news/PDFs/sob05.pdf.

9. Personal communication, December 2006. A warden for the BOP only stays at a single institution for an average of about 18 months, whereas TDCJ wardens serve much longer tenures. There has been one major exception to this, with Warden Hood at ADX-Florence, who served for nearly five years, although this is not surprising given the specialized nature of the administrative maximum facility.

10. Some of the prison officials that I talked to felt that this feeling of "being held to a different standard" was made worse by the fact that they wore a uniform and worked for the state.

11. Harrison, *The First Casualty: Violence against Women in Canadian Military Communities.*

12. Jacobs, *Statesville: The Penitentiary in Mass Society.* DiIulio, *Governing Prisons: A Case Study of Correctional Management.* Riveland, "Prison Management Trends, 1975–2025."

13. Court intervention has also been part of the need for this. See Feeley and Rubin, *Judicial Policy-Making and the Modern State: How the Courts Reformed America's Prisons.* DiIulio, "Crime and Punishment in Wisconsin."

14. For example, the BOP has 19 maximum-security institutions across the country.

15. The entire handbook can be found at http://www.tdcj.state.tx.us/publications/cid/OffendOrientHbkNov04.pdf, retrieved on January 3, 2007.

16. http://www.tdcj.state.tx.us/publications/cid/GR-106%20Web%20Final%20doc%203-23-05.pdf, retrieved on January 3, 2007

17. Conover, *Newjack: Guarding Sing Sing.* DiIulio, *Governing Prisons: A Case Study of Correctional Management.* Jacobs, *Statesville: The Penitentiary in Mass Society.* Lin, *Reform in the Making: The Implementation of Social Policy in Prison.*

18. DiIulio, *Governing Prisons: A Case Study of Correctional Management.* Jacobs, *Statesville: The Penitentiary in Mass Society*, 13.

19. Jacobs, *Statesville: The Penitentiary in Mass Society*. McGee, *Prisons and Politics*.

20. DiIulio comes up with a three-pronged typology of prison management: the control model, the responsibility model, and the consensual model. He concludes that the Texas control model ultimately leads to the safest prisons. For a critique of his typology and methodology, see Simon, "The 'Society of Captives' in the Era of Hyper-Incarceration."

21. Lin, *Reform in the Making: The Implementation of Social Policy in Prison*. Useem et al., *States of Siege: U.S. Prison Riots, 1971–1986*.

22. Jacobs, *Statesville: The Penitentiary in Mass Society*. DiIulio, *Governing Prisons: A Case Study of Correctional Management*. Wright, "The World of Work Has Changed! So What Does This Mean for Correctional Management?"

23. Several people that I interviewed in Texas told me that when they talked to Doug Dretke, the former director of the TDCJ's Correctional Institutions division, he always asks them if they are taking classes and if not, why not.

24. Wright, "The World of Work Has Changed! So What Does This Mean for Correctional Management?", 199.

25. Wright, "The World of Work Has Changed! So What Does This Mean for Correctional Management?" Feeley et al., *Judicial Policy-Making and the Modern State: How the Courts Reformed America's Prisons*. DiIulio, "Crime and Punishment in Wisconsin." http://thesconz.wordpress.com/2009/09/22/crime-and-punishment-in-wisconsin/.

26. Blumstein, "Prisons," in *Crime*, edited by James Q. Wilson and Joan Petersilia.

27. Wright, "The World of Work Has Changed! So What Does This Mean for Correctional Management?", 199–200.

28. Turn on MSNBC on any given weekend and you will see a variety of shows shot inside of prisons around the country.

29. Personal communication, January 2004.

30. Wright, "The World of Work Has Changed! So What Does This Mean for Correctional Management?"

31. *Ibid.*

32. Personal communication, February 2004.

33. Thomas Jefferson to James Madison, ME 11: 351, 1807.

34. Obviously there will be some overlap in these categories, but this should not detract from the categorization as a useful tool in understanding prison administrators' behavior in this arena.

35. I am left to wonder how much their external behavior correlates to how they run the institution themselves. I found it particularly interesting how many of the wardens who fit into my citizen category were practitioners of DiIulio's "management by walking around." DiIulio, *Governing Prisons: A Case Study of Correctional Management*.

36. Personal communication, February 2004.

37. Personal communication, January 2004.

38. Personal communication, February 2004.

39. Personal communication, February 2004. There is often good reason to stay out of the local political scene. In the towns I studied, local politics is a blood sport. I heard stories of a gun being pulled on a political rival, a mayor threatening to jump over the desk to get at someone at a city council meeting, and a city councilor who refuses to ever vote on the record because it would mean he was giving his tacit consent to the system.

40. Personal communication, July 2003.

41. National Institute of Corrections, 1992.

42. Even after the advent of the Prison Litigation Reform Act of 1995, which sought to limit so-called frivolous inmates' lawsuits through various administrative measures, federal district courts still get an enormous amount of filings from prisons. Over 31 percent of the cases on those courts' civil dockets were about prison issues in 2005. This issue and its effect on the communities in my study are discussed in chapter five, http://www.uscourts.gov/caseload2005/tables/C02mar05.pdf.

43. This is actually not uncommon, and several scholars have noted this phenomenon. Jacobs, *New Perspectives on Prisons and Imprisonment*. McShane et al.,"Prison Impact Studies: Some Comments on Methodological Rigor." Krause, "Community Opposition to Correctional Facility Siting: Beyond the NIMBY Syndrome."

44. Personal communication, July 2003.

45. Personal communication, October 2006.

46. Personal communication, October 2006.

47. Eisinger, *The Rise of the Entrepreneurial State: State and Local Economic Development Policy in the United States*.

Chapter Five

The Community's Story

Local economic development is a practical concept to strengthen the economic capacity of a locality to improve its future and the quality of life for all. It focuses on local competitive advantages and provides communities with the means to identify new opportunities to create jobs and income.

Juan Somavia, Director-General, ILO

I don't know that siting prisons for economic reasons is good for the community or the prisons.

Dana Hendrick, Director of Probation and Parole,
San Patricio County, Texas

In her 1980 state of the state address, Dixie Lee Ray, then-governor of Washington, announced that a new 500-bed medium-security prison would be built in Monroe, Washington. This was news to the people who lived in Monroe (which already housed the Washington State Reformatory) and who were not looking to get a second prison in their midst. The town sued the state to stop the building of the prison, and after a lengthy negotiation process, Monroe allowed the state to build a prison there, but in return, they were given money for improvements to local schools and utilities. Just 10 years later, most states were finding a much more receptive audience to house their inmates, with a "prison derby" of sorts developing in which various communities lobby the government to site a prison in their community.[1]

This chapter focuses on how community actors relate to the prison once it is opened. Much of this relationship is set during the lobbying process, and the communities in this study both tell a story of economic woe and hopes that the prison will be the savior. The story told by the community is one of met and unmet expectations by the institution brought in to save them. The beginnings of the story are told in terms of the two most important commodities that these communities hope the prison will provide—jobs and housing. These two issues are of great importance to the local community, and how they are dealt with will have great influence on the relationship that develops. The rest of the story is about the relationship developed and the problems of the "outsider" as seen from the community's standpoint.

There are two factors involved. The first has to do with the kind of relationship that develops between the community and the prison, be it a formal one or an informal one, and how the type of relationship fits their needs. Additionally, no matter how many jobs go to locals, a significant percentage of the employees will be coming in from other facilities. This influx of newcomers is a difficult part of this process for the community to handle, and we begin to see the emergence of the dichotomy between insiders and outsiders.

During the lobbying and siting process, expectations grow as to the numbers of jobs that will be coming with the prison and who will be getting them. The state and federal governments raise these expectations during this time, but their respective ability to deliver differs greatly. The different hiring practices between the two entities leads to many more locals being hired by the state facilities in Beeville as compared with the federal facilities in Florence.

This leads to the second issue—that of housing. This issue has two parts. First is the preparedness of the town itself for the potential impact of new people wanting to move to the community. In this regard, Beeville was far better prepared than Florence. Regardless of these preparations, the hiring practice seems to matter more. More of the Texas Department of Criminal Justice (TDCJ)'s employees seem willing to move to Beeville than federal employees are to move to Florence. This may be because of the more "cosmopolitan" nature of federal employees, but it may also be that state jobs are more likely to be filled by Texans, who are more likely to feel comfortable in and move to the area.

The third issue is about the type of relationship developed by these two different entities. The Bureau of Prisons (BOP) has garnered a more formal relationship with the community, one in which community concerns do not have an opportunity to come to the forefront. The more informal relationship garnered by the state may be a product of the less bureaucratic nature of state governmental organizations as opposed to federal ones. Despite the differences, both communities struggle with the influx of outsiders to their small communities, and even here we see the state doing a more effective job in overcoming these problems. Rural communities are somewhat closed communities, and the acceptance of "the outsider" in the form of new prison employees is difficult. State employees are at least from similar communities and seem to have an easier time being accepted. As such, the prisons in Beeville have become, for better and worse, a part of the community, whereas Florence's prisons stay somewhat apart from the town.[2]

THE EXPECTATIONS GAME

The community's expectations of what the prison will bring and the reality of what it does bring are a vital part of the perception of success and the eventual relationship that is worked out. The most important of these expectations has to do with jobs. Jobs are the holy grail of the prison game (and local economic development generally) and knowing what kind and how many jobs will actually go to locals is difficult to measure in advance. Even so, Beeville seems to have been more prepared by the state as to what exactly they were getting. This section discusses the expectations raised during the lobbying process and the institutional factors that get in the way of meeting those expectations.

During the lobbying process, both sides attempt to put their best proposals forward, but once the construction begins and the prison gates are opened (or closed, I suppose), the proposals become a thing of the past. From the community's perspective, after the prison opens, they come to grips with what they will and will not receive as benefits. Here we begin to see the difference between the federal government and the state. The federal government's hiring practices are much more stringent, and many more local residents in Beeville were able to get jobs at the state facility than Florence residents were at the federal facilities.

Even the most optimistic prison systems only promise that 60 percent of jobs will go to local citizens, so many of the employees will inevitably come in from the outside. This influx of new people is a shock to a small town. But given the atmosphere surrounding the prison derby, it is not difficult to see how this process might lead to some confusion down the line. The replacement of the DAD (decide, announce, defend) model with the LLC (lobby, lobby, celebrate) model is at the heart of the problem. In the "not in my backyard" (NIMBY) era, prison officials had to lobby as hard as they did because communities could be expected to fight the proposal to put a prison in their backyard. But because this is no longer the case, it has become impossible to determine who is doing the selling and who is doing the buying, with both sides continuously upping the stakes and promising to move the process along.

In essence, both sides are doing the selling in this process; therefore, no one is viewing the process with a critical eye. Promises are left unanalyzed and questions are not asked. We will see below that although "X number of jobs" promises are consistently made, there is no examination of how many qualified people actually reside in the community. There is little discussion of the prisons' buying procedures, an important factor because many communities assume that the prisons will shop locally, and there is little interest in the mounting evidence that there will be little or no impact on the economy. Both sides become so involved in the pitch that the reality of what is to come never really enters into the discussion.

SO YOU WANT TO BE A PRISON GUARD

On average, security jobs make up over 90 percent of the staff at any prison facility. This means that most jobs available to local workers are the low-paying and high-stress jobs as corrections officers (COs). Even those can be difficult to get. These are government jobs with good benefits and pension plans. There may be other jobs at a facility that are within reach of locals (e.g., certain office jobs), but the CO positions are the plum jobs.[3] This section will focus on the hiring of COs in these communities and analyze how expectations and reality failed to meet in either community. I will further discuss the difference between the BOP's hiring practices and the TDCJ's. I will end the section with a brief discussion of the difficulty of the job of the CO and how that has tapped the local labor market and forced the prisons to look elsewhere for employees.

In newspaper reports leading up to the opening of the prison in Florence, a figure of 60 percent was often mentioned as the number of prison jobs that would go to local residents. In a speech in front of the local chamber of commerce, Gary Stendahl, a contracting officer for the BOP, claimed that, "approximately 40 percent of the permanent staff are expected to be transferred here from other facilities, with the remaining to be hired locally."[4] Another newspaper article quotes Whitney Leblanc, the deputy chief of the National Recruiting Office, pointing out that prison jobs would be more than just COs. "We need stockmen and warehousers. The vast majority of entry-level jobs, we want to hire from this community. That's the whole purpose of our coming here."[5] He reiterated that approximately 60 percent of jobs would go to locals, but he did not mention how few of these non-security-related jobs there really were. "We want this community to play an awesome part in the staffing of this institution," he added. At that time, the staff needed was estimated at 900, meaning 540 jobs were assumed to be coming to a community of just over 3,000 residents. Another newspaper report put the number of proposed jobs at "between 750 and 900."[6]

However, residents were disappointed when they came to realize the limits on the BOP's hiring practices, although they were told of them up front. There was an age restriction and an examination that prospects had to pass to be considered.[7] Additionally, according to the BOP Web site, successful candidates must have completed one of the following:

A full 4-year course of study in any field leading to a Bachelor's Degree from an accredited school or possession of a Bachelor's Degree; or the equivalent of at least 3 years of full-time general experience performing duties such as providing assistance, guidance, and direction to individuals; counseling individuals; responding to emergency situations; supervising or managing; teaching or instructing individuals; or selling products or services (persuasive commissioned sales); or a combination of undergraduate education and general experience equivalent to 3 years of full-time experience.[8]

Taken as a whole, this means that prospects for many residents were not good. In 2000, only 13.1 percent of Florence residents had received a bachelor's degree.[9] To have the three-years' experience that the federal government required, applicants would need to be between the ages of roughly 21 and 35. Census data show that there were only 427 residents of Florence who even met the age requirements for the job, much less the other prerequisites.[10]

This is where the expectations failed to meet reality. In all of the discussions about numbers of jobs for locals, no one seems to have pointed out how few local citizens would actually qualify for positions at the prison. Only approximately 36 Florence residents could possibly have met the age and the educational requirement, and of the remaining 391 people who met the age requirement, how many of those would meet the other requirements for those without a degree? Even county wide, only approximately 600 people met the degree and age requirements for the BOP in 1990.[11] Of those, how many would actually need to go to work at the prison, even if a job were available to them?

For those who did make the cut and could handle the stress of the job, the payoff was relatively good. The current starting pay rate for an incoming CO in Florence is $28,349 a year, significantly more than the per capita income of the county, which was $17,420 for the year 2000 Census. It is also quite a bit more than the Colorado Department of Corrections (CDOC) currently pays ($21,756 for new officers). A Bureau of Labor Statistics study also shows the median income of a federal CO to be much more than that of state employees nationwide, with BOP officers earning $44,700, whereas the median income for all states was just $33,750.[12]

There is a hierarchy of job placements according to many residents of both communities.[13] People spoke not only of the better pay that federal employees get, but also a better class of inmates ("cream of the crap" was how one officer put it) and many more programs for inmates. However, despite the better jobs offered by the BOP, Florence may not have done itself any favors by going after a federal prison rather than a state facility. State jobs are much easier to get; therefore, Beeville was able to have more locals go to work for their newly landed industry because the TDCJ's standards are considerably less stringent, but they also do not pay as well. The starting salary for a Texas CO is just over $21,000.

The TDCJ requires applicants only to have a General Educational Development (GED) or high school diploma and be 18 years of age. The requirements also include

- You must never have been convicted of a felony.
- You must never have been convicted of a drug-related offense.
- You must never have been convicted of an offense involving domestic violence.

- You cannot have had a Class A or B misdemeanor conviction within the past five years.
- You cannot be on probation for any criminal offense.
- You cannot have any criminal charges pending or have an outstanding warrant.

There is also short test, which includes[14]

- Memory and observation—four questions
- Situational reasoning—four questions
- Reading comprehension/deductive reasoning—two questions
- Verbal reasoning—four questions
- Arithmetic—six questions

It is easier for the TDCJ to hire locals, and most people claim that they have done so. Neither department keeps records as to how many jobs actually go to locals, but all of the anecdotal evidence seems to indicate that Beeville reaped much greater benefits in this regard. Both communities were expecting the magic number of 60 percent of jobs to go to locals, and although no one thinks either community got close to that figure, Beeville certainly came closer.

In addition to problems with numbers of locals hired, the job of CO itself is an extremely difficult one. Potential applicants may or may not have been aware of this difficulty. The high stress rate among COs has been well documented.[15] Evidence indicates that high levels of stress on the job have led to high turnover rates and high rates of sick leave as well as troubled relationships with other staff and families. Several other studies showed similar problems in other areas of the country.[16]

Because of the difficulty of the job, turnover in any prison, especially a maximum-security institution, is enormous, and the local labor pool gets tapped fairly quickly. The TDCJ has been bussing people from Corpus Christi (70 miles away) and even San Antonio (120 miles away) to fill the labor shortfall. Even so, the McConnell Unit in Beeville is consistently understaffed, not because of a lack of locals who want jobs, but a lack of locals who are qualified and can handle the job. Another 2,250-bed unit has also opened in Carnes County next door, complicating things even further. According to one of my sources, the TDCJ has actually relaxed its already low standards in some rural areas to fill positions.[17]

The BOP does not seem to have as severe staffing issues as the TDCJ (at least at three of the Florence facilities),[18] but this is, in part, due to the way they hire their employees. When applying for a job as a CO, candidates are allowed to rank which institutions would be preferable to them to work in, but no guarantees are made. Training takes place in Georgia, and applicants are told that moving may well be a requirement for the job, especially if they want to move up the ranks. This may also lead to the federal employees' disinterest in really laying down roots.

Jobs may be the name of the game in local economic development, but the TDCJ and the BOP seem to play this game very differently. The promise of who will be in the starting lineup seems to be the same for both entities, but who will actually be given the ball is very different. The gap between the promise of jobs and reality of who will be hired leads to the second major issue from the community's standpoint— that of housing. This is also a product of expectations not always meeting reality.

SO YOU WANT TO LIVE IN A PRISON TOWN

Housing is the second major issue that affects the relationship from the community's standpoint. Because the prison does not pay property taxes (and does not tend to buy products locally), new housing is one of the best ways for a town to make money from the prison. There are two separate considerations in this regard that matter. First, the town needs to have an available stock of housing for new employees. Second, and perhaps more importantly, the prisons need to hire people willing to move to their community. Whether prison employees will want to relocate to an area has two components: the social needs of the employees and the racial makeup of the community.

Housing for new employees was not much of an issue in Beeville, especially after the naval air station closed and additional affordable housing became available. In fact, the TDCJ did a study of the living patterns of two of the three prisons in town and found that out of 1,156 employees working at the unit in 2002, 656 lived in Beeville, or 56.7 percent of the prison's employees.[19] Another study by the Human Resources Office of the TDCJ stated that as of January 2003, there were 1,802 TDCJ employees working in the county. Of those, 1,111 lived within county limits, 61.6 percent of all employees.

This has not been so simple for Florence. Although the community may expect to get jobs, the prison expects the community to have affordable housing for its employees. One warden for the BOP told me that he heard that the town thought that the BOP had a requirement that upper-level employees live within a small radius of the institution to be able to respond to emergencies quickly. The BOP has no such policy. Whether or not this was true is, in some ways, beside the point. If locals thought this might be the case, it would have been very simple to find out for sure by asking the BOP. No one did, and most upper-level officials in Florence choose to live elsewhere.[20]

The executive director of the Florence Chamber of Commerce, Darryl Lindsay, claims that the town was not prepared for the influx of people and the housing markets could not sustain the demand.[21] He says that the town was (and still is) badly in need of rental housing for the BOP employees, who transfer every 18 months or so. They also were not prepared for the housing crunch that would come with the new employees, and they lost a lot of people to Pueblo West and Colorado Springs. Lindsay agrees that some of the minority employees lived elsewhere "to be with their own" as he puts it. He calls this "voluntary segregation."[22] Local building contractors did not have the money to build, and some people, who he calls the "social employees," were going to live in a bigger city anyway. These social employees wanted nightclubs, sporting events, and such, things that Florence and Fremont County lack.

What Lindsay fails to point out is that there is another thing that Florence lacks—people of color. Community residents and prison personnel all seem to agree that very few minority prison workers chose to move to Florence. Pueblo and Colorado Springs have significant minority populations, and although there is no hard evidence of this, most interviewees claimed that black prison employees move to Colorado Springs and Hispanics go to Pueblo or Pueblo West, which is even closer to Florence.[23] One African American former warden at the federal prison told a local community leader that he had to go to Colorado Springs just to get a haircut because no one in town knew what to do with his hair. Several community leaders pointed out how much there was a racial component to how many commuters the BOP has. According to the BOP, 21 percent of its staff nationwide is African American and 11.3 percent is Hispanic. This is a significant number of potential residents lost to other communities.

Florence mayor Tom McCormick and 24 other community leaders actually made a trip to Sheridan, Oregon, to see what the impact of a federal prison had been on the local community there. This trip was made after the prison derby had ended and Florence had been chosen as the site for a new federal facility. Sheridan is a community roughly the size of Florence that had also lobbied to land a federal facility. According to one newspaper report, all involved were very impressed with the prison and its effect on the town, but the group does not appear to have dug very deep. McCormick stated that, "he was also impressed with the fact that some local people were hired by the FBP (Federal Bureau of Prisons). He said that he didn't find out how many of the 286 people employed by the FBP are local, but there are 60 families living in Sheridan."[24]

It would seem that there were two problems with this trip. First, it took place after the prison had already begun construction, not while the town was considering courting the prison system in the first place. At that point, there was little that could be done if there were any potential problems. The second problem is the lack of any depth in the questioning by community leaders of the leaders of Sheridan. In speaking to one of the community leaders who made the trip, he stated that the main focus of the group's questions was housing prices. The town leaders of Sheridan told them not to just jack up housing prices, expecting that BOP employees would just pay it. They failed to even follow this advice and failed to ask for any detail about other issues that might come up or enough detail on the issues that were discussed. "Some" jobs going to locals is a far cry from "most" jobs. Community leaders seem to have been caught up in prison fever and did not ask the kinds of questions that the town's residents needed to know.

In terms of housing, Beeville might have benefited from its location in a way that Florence could not. A California study of its own prison towns concluded, "it is relatively rare for the small host cities less than 100 miles from urban cities to be the preferred location for staff to live."[25] The report found that, in essence, the farther away a prison town was from an urban area, the more likely it was to have the prison's employees live in the host community. The report does not analyze why this might be the case, but the findings alone are important. Although both towns in my study have metropolitan areas within a 100-mile radius, Florence has two cities much closer that seem to drain BOP employees. Pueblo, with population of more than 100,000 people, is 30 miles away, and Colorado Springs, with more than 350,000 people,[26] is within 45 miles. Both cities are a fairly easy commute, and many employees seem content to make it.[27] On the other hand, Corpus Christi, a city of 277,000, is 60 miles from Beeville, a much longer commute. Additionally, the

TDCJ has done an admirable job of pleasing the large percentage of Hispanic Beeville residents by placing many Hispanics in positions of power in the prison. They claim that they have not planned it that way, but regardless, it seems to have helped.

FORMALITY?

Although the basics for the relationship between community and prison seem to be set up during the lobbying process and soon after the prison opens, over time, the community in these two towns have developed two different types of relationships with the prison: formal or informal.[28] In these two cases, it is the informal one that seems to be best for the community, in which community leaders have a strong, almost friendly bond with the prison administration. In Beeville, there are no formal meetings between the town and prison administrators, but instead, the lines of communications are open and used as needed. The way the relationship has grown over time has led to this. The wardens at the prisons are easy for the town officials to contact and this accessibility has been mostly positive. For example, Bob Horn, former sheriff of Bee County, often went to the McConnell Unit to have coffee with the warden and just "visit."

However, the relationship goes much deeper. The city council and county commission each has a member who works or has worked at the prison. Although neither politician is particularly high up in the prison food chain (upper-level prison employees are barred from getting involved in politics), they both have contacts in the prison and a strong understanding of the inner workings of the facility. Gil Herrera, a city councilman, goes to work at the prison on a daily basis, sees what is going on, and has intimate knowledge of potential problems when they arise.[29] Carlos Salazar, a county commissioner, used to work full time for the prison and still picks up shifts as a part-time CO. Salazar's wife also works there.[30] Additionally, TDCJ hired former Beeville Chief of Police Bill Lazeby to work in its investigations unit. This type of crossover has helped their strong working relationship.

I asked several officials in Beeville if they wished they had formal community meetings with prison officials and none seemed to think that they were necessary. Ford Patton, the city manager of Beeville, felt that the more informal way of doing business was much better, at least in their case: "I tend to believe that the lines of communication between TDCJ and other entities are open enough as is," Patton explained to me.[31] He added that everyone involved was very busy, and that an extra meeting was not important or wanted by anyone.

South Texas is a handshake and backslap kind of place, and informality in relationships may come naturally. Although one might assume that this explains Beeville's relationship with the TDCJ, Florence also has an informal, small-town feel to it. It might further be assumed that a rural community such as this would have no problem building an informal relationship with its biggest industry, but this has not been the case. The informal relationship that has been worked out in Beeville is unquestionably closer than the more formal one in Florence, where the prison holds scheduled, quarterly meetings with community leaders. It may be that without the formal community relations meetings there would be no face-to-face contact at all between prison and community in Florence, but I would argue that it leads officials to feel that no other contact needs to be made, given that there will be a meeting at which issues can be discussed. These meetings take place at a different facility each time and have a set agenda with a lunch afterward. I attended only a few of these meetings, so I cannot generalize, but the head of the local chamber of commerce told me that the meetings I attended were typical.

For example, at one of these meetings, several important community members, including the local chief of police, were not in attendance, and the need to increase membership was an important topic on the agenda. Additionally, the senior warden of only one of four facilities was there, and associate wardens represented the rest of the facilities. The main focus of the meeting was the community-service projects taken on by the inmates of the minimum-security prison (the prison woodshop made a sign for a local park) and inmate work programs inside of the other federal facilities. In the past, the prison had helped with improvements at the local school, renovations on the Rialto Theater in downtown, and work at the Colorado State Veteran's Home. UNICOR, the BOP's industrial division, donated chairs to the local school system and they were making a new sign for a local park.

What was striking was how unaware the general public seems to be as to these projects in Florence. These projects are vital to showing a community the added benefits of a prison in the community. In Beeville, the community-service squads were discussed by nearly everyone I interviewed, but the same could hardly be said of Florence. It may be that the service squads are less visible in Florence than in

Beeville because I never saw inmates from the federal prison working in Florence, but I saw several TDCJ work crews in Beeville during my time there.

Although these formal meetings are supposed to be a forum in which there is an open discussion between community leaders and prison officials, the meeting felt more like a continued sales pitch by the BOP as to how much the prison is doing for its inmates and the community. Additionally, the BOP sets the agenda for the meeting, although community leaders can request to have issues added. One such attempt at agenda-setting by a community leader shows how tightly the BOP controls information. This man tried to have the issue of domestic violence put on the agenda for one of the advisory council meetings. Instead of it being put on the agenda, the man was summoned to a meeting with the wardens of the various federal facilities. Their employees questioned him as to how he knew about the domestic violence, and the man was then accused of having some sort of confidential information. They refused to put the issue on the agenda, stating that they had no problem with domestic violence and that it was an internal matter. The issue did not make the agenda.

It is interesting that in the community (Beeville) with no formal meeting mechanism to force parties together, the lines of communication between prison and town are so much stronger. This is, in part, a function of federal prison versus state, which is discussed further below, but it is also related to how relations have been worked out from the start. The fact that the TDCJ hired more local people and seems to do more to keep its people actively involved in the local community has obviously helped, but Beeville's leaders have also taken an active role in fostering this relationship. The town of Florence has been more passive in its relationship with the BOP.

So why does the informal relationship work so much better? It may not be that one type of relationship is better in all cases, but instead follows what the rest of this research suggests, that the building of relationships with the local community is more of a priority for the state government, whereas it is not as important for the federal government. One reason for this may be related to the hiring practices and the feeling of the federal employee as outsider, in their own minds and that of the community.

With more local people working at the TDCJ's prisons, there are obviously going to be more opportunities for casual relationships with members of the community that may lead to a better understanding of the local community. Without question, having local elected officials who also work at the prison (or who have worked there in the past) will help foster a better working relationship. Prisons are a nearly closed society, one that is mysterious and often misunderstood. Whether it is the high ranking employees who work at the prison or politicians like County Commissioner Carlos Salazar who work there, the Beeville community has more linkages to the inside of this closed society. Having the ability to hire local community members is an obvious advantage to the TDCJ in this regard.

Even so, from the community of Florence's standpoint, very few of the BOP employees have reached out to them.[32] Discussions with community residents and leaders often focused on this fact. With a few exceptions, community members felt like they had hoped to find a partner with which to work, but instead they found an entity that was mostly closed to them.[33] The federal bureaucracy has been too overwhelming to wade through, and with just the Community Relations Board's quarterly meetings as a way to have their concerns heard, there is little hope that this will change. The next section will discuss this issue in more detail and lay the groundwork for the argument that the state is more responsive politically than the federal government.

INSIDERS AND OUTSIDERS

The opening of a prison requires a large influx of experienced personnel, regardless of how many prison jobs go to locals. This invasion of the outsider seems to be the catch-22 of economic development strategy for rural communities—they want the jobs that the new industry will bring local citizens, but they do not want the new influx of people that inevitably come with it. One Florence resident claimed that she could pick out a "fed pen" employee walking down the street. "They aren't as friendly and don't seem to want to be part of the community. They have their own softball teams, with professional uniforms and everything."[34] This sentiment (although not the uniform comment) was one I often heard around town. BOP employees were perceived as transients who would be transferred in a few years or moved when they got promoted.

The same things are not said as much about TDCJ employees. Those who moved to the area came to stay, not as a stop on the way to greener pastures. Beeville seems to have been more prepared for the influx of people to their community, and this preparation has paid off. This is not to say that there are not problems. In discussing the criminal and family problems among the prison employees, local community members in Beeville often use an "us versus them" vocabulary. For example, Jim Miller, the superintendent of the Beeville Independent School District, made a distinction between local students who got in trouble and the children of COs who did the same.[35]

Some of this is odd in Beeville because they have some experience with outsiders who come into town for work. Naval Air Station–Chase Field used to be the largest employer in the town, and naval personnel were constantly being shuffled in and out. Ten years after the base closed and the McConnell Unit opened, the comparisons between the base and its employees and the TDCJ are constant. When a base closes, each level of government has a "right of first refusal" to use the land. The town of Beeville had hoped to build an industrial park, but the state government was higher up on the totem pole and chose to grab the land surrounding the old administration buildings for the TDCJ. There seems to be some resentment in the community over this land grab.

In some ways, the TDCJ has been a better neighbor to the town than the Navy was, although the perception is not necessarily so. People often talk about the naval employees of being a better "class" than TDCJ workers, but as Mayor Ken Cheshir points out, "[W]e had problems with the swabbies [navy enlisted men] as well, but people around here just remember the naval aviators driving their sports cars around, not the enlisted men who got drunk and fought with 'townies.'"[36] Regardless of people's feelings, the prison system may have saved the town. Joe Montez argues that, "we lost 2,100 jobs but we gained about 1,000, so the effect (of the base closing) wasn't as devastating as it might have been."[37]

Additionally, TDCJ employees are more likely than naval aviators to become a part of the community. Cheshir says,

> The TDCJ employees spend their money here in town, whereas the navy folks used to use the base commissary. I think that the county payroll has been cut in half, but they seem to be more a part of the community than the navy officers were. The navy aviators and their wives were educated and wanted to go to Corpus to socialize. A lot of the TDCJ employees also just work

here, but there are those, that one in a hundred person, who really sets down roots here and becomes active in the community.[38]

It is that one-in-a-hundred person that these towns really hope for, and Beeville seems to have gotten its wish to a greater extent than Florence. Beeville may not always be happy with the employees who come to town, and the prison was far from a perfect solution to all of their problems, but the prison and its employees have become a part of the community. Those who have become a part of their community and a part of their political system have mitigated the notion of the outsider invading their town. There is very little such crossover in Florence.

However, Florence's problems go deeper than the fact that the BOP is not buying hammers at Jim's Hardware on Main Street or that prison employees choose to live elsewhere. A community-assessment report by the Colorado Office of Economic Development and International Trade points out several issues in the community, which included

- Prison town perception
- Lack of business growth
- Perception that upper management at federal prisons live some-where else
- Lack of jobs for spouses (of prison employees)
- Lack of housing for new higher-end employees (of the prison)
- Retail businesses appear not to have adapted to current consumer behaviors
- Chemical and substance abuse[39]

Problems as widespread as these are not solvable by getting the prison to buy chicken from Skyline Superfoods or by getting more residents who work there. The problems show the need for two major commodities that Florence lacks: good affordable housing and local ancillary industry that provides jobs for local families.[40]

Many community officials pointed out one other problem to me. The report lists "political barriers: Florence versus Cañon attitude" as one of the town's major weaknesses. In essence, this boils down to the fact that the communities are in competition with each other—politically, socially, and especially economically. Although this is just one of a myriad of weaknesses (some strengths are listed as well), this one area seems to be of great importance locally. One local official put it more succinctly. "Florence is like Cañon's ugly little stepbrother."[41]

It is interesting that the little brother would choose the same path to economic growth as the older brother, but with a very different entity (the federal government) and with very different results. The choice to become a prison town and court the Federal BOP, thereby giving Fremont County more prisons than any other county in the nation, no doubt had to do with Cañon City's long history with prisons. In fact, the East Cañon Complex, home to six Colorado state facilities, bumps up against Florence's western edge.

These problems of the insider and outsider seem to be endemic in rural communities.[42] Large cities can handle a large influx of people without much trouble, but in a town with a population of a small college, this is not the case. The state employees and leaders seemed to understand the nature of rural communities better and the importance of getting involved in their host community. Although the federal government developed a more formal relationship that might work well in a large city, the state seemed to understand that this was not the best course of action. In the next section, we will see how the abovementioned issues have led to the current state of the relationship from the community's standpoint and the consequences of the informal relationship that has developed in Beeville and the formal one in Florence.

CONCLUSIONS

The impact of a prison on a community from the community's point of view is the one part of this research that has been looked at to some extent by the available literature.[43] What has not garnered attention is the relationship that develops between prison and town after the facility is in place. Several large issues seem to show up in both communities: expectations, jobs, housing, and the type of relationship that ends up developing.

The issue of expectations forms during the lobbying stage and follows through all of the stages of development. Given the end of the NIMBY model and the fact that prison systems now have their pick of small towns in which to site their facilities, the prison should be able to give more realistic estimates of job prospects and housing needs. Additionally, the community needs to be realistic as to what it can provide in terms of employees and housing opportunities. Florence, which has had bigger problems in the housing area, has just seen a new moderate- to upper-scale housing development built in town, but it is yet to be seen whether or not this will convince federal employees to move to town.

The type of relationship that develops may or may not have much influence on how strong that working relationship will be. Formal mechanisms that force meetings between top prison officials and community leaders are not an inherently bad thing, but these meetings need to be an open forum to really air concerns, not a show put on by the prison system. Agenda-setting should be open to both sides, and senior wardens should be required to attend. This alone might make the community take these meetings more seriously, leading to better community participation.

When an informal relationship develops between the prison and the community, as is the case in Beeville, there appears to be more openness and more opportunities for the prison to have a positive effect on the town. To develop this relationship, both sides need to be willing to put in the effort. Treating prison workers who move to the community as outsiders does not help, and recognizing the type of workers the town is getting is important. Beeville's tendency to focus on what prison employees are not (i.e., not naval officers) rather than what they are can be problematic. Additionally, there seems to be a tendency to forget the problems that naval people brought, as pointed out by Mayor Ken Cheshir, and a lack of focus on the things that prison employees do (e.g., put down long-term roots and shop locally, rather than on the base). But the prison's employees do cause some problems that sometimes involve the police. It is the relationship between the police and the prison that will be the focus of the next chapter.

NOTES

1. Personal communication, January 2004. Susan Stasny, a county commissioner in Bee County, Texas, was the first person I heard use the term "prison derby."

2. Hervé Varenne discusses this "insider" and "outsider" dichotomy extensively in his work *Americans Together* (1977).

3. The other really good jobs at any prison are going to be in the medical sector, but the TDCJ and BOP use outside contractors for these jobs. Also, all of the staff at these facilities had to meet the same requirements that are expected of the potential COs. These requirements are discussed below.

4. *Wet Mountain Tribune,* June 21, 1990.

5. *Ibid.,* 3A.

6. *Ibid.*

7. New employees at the time had to be under the age of 35. This restriction has since been raised to 37.

8. http://www.bop.gov/jobs/job_descriptions/correctional_officer.jsp.

9. http://www.census.gov/prod/2002pubs/00ccdb/cc00_tabB5.pdf.

10. http://www.dola.state.co.us/Demog/Census/DemogProfiles/1600827040.pdf.

11. http://www.dola.state.co.us/Demog/Census/DemogProfiles/Fremont.pdf.

12. Private prison employees fare far worse, with a median salary of just $21,490, less than the starting salaries of both states' systems and far below the starting salary for the BOP. http://www.bls.gov/oco/ocos156.htm.

13. Beeville also has a federal prison, FCI Three Rivers, within commuting distance, and both towns have private prisons within 40 miles. Private prisons are easily on the bottom of the food chain.

14. Feel free to take a sample test yourself at http://www.tdcj.state.tx.us/vacancy/coinfo/test/info.htm.

15. Launay and Fielding, "Stress Among Prison Officers: Some Empirical Evidence Based on Self Report," 138–148.

16. Whitehead and Lindquist, "Correctional Officer Job Burnout: A Path Model," 23–42.

17. Personal communication, March 2004.

18. There have been consistent complaints from the federal CO employees union about understaffing problems at the ADX.

19. Bee Development Authority, study of labor commuting patterns. Given to the author by Joe Montez.

20. The BOP has ignored repeated requests for data on housing patterns of employees at FCC–Florence, arguing that it is a security issue, so the evidence for Florence is anecdotal.

21. Personal communication, August 2003.

22. Personal communication, August 2003.

23. All of my interviewees made reference to this. There is no way to match racial characteristics with zip codes without violating the confidentiality of the employees, but because I do not even have access to the zip codes, the point is moot.

24. *Cañon City Daily Record,* May 4, 1990.

25. Bureau of Equalization, (2002) 10.

26. On the basis of 2000 Census figures.

27. One warden explained to me that many of his employees were from high-traffic areas on the East Coast, so a long commute to work was not a problem.

28. There is actually a third relationship that I have heard about but have not seen firsthand: no relationship. Because I did not study such a town, I cannot discuss this possibility in any meaningful way here. However, it also seems that the expectations game in stage two leads to the "no relationship" model in the same way the formal versus informal model has.

29. Personal communication, March 2004.

30. Personal communication, February 2004.

31. Personal communication, January 2004.

32. The exceptions to this are discussed in the prison management chapter.

33. Community members might, under other circumstances, be willing to deal with this, but next door is an example of a very different type of relationship, the very cozy relationship between the CDOC and Cañon City. In fact, Florence's highest-ranking home-grown prison employee is a woman named Cathy Slack, a Florence native and still a resident who is currently the assistant warden at the Colorado State Penitentiary.

34. Personal communication, June 2003.

35. Personal communication, January 2004. This reiterates the fear-versus-reality issue when it comes to prison communities. Although they fear the inmate's families before the prison opens, it is the COs and their families that actually become the source of trouble.

36. Personal communication, January 2004.

37. Personal communication, January 2004.

38. Personal communication, January 2004.

39. COEDIT, 2004.

40. Even Florence's larger next-door neighbor Cañon City provides little industry as such, because by far the largest employer in town is the CDOC.

41. Personal communication, July 2003.

42. Varenne, *Americans Together: Structured Diversity in a Midwestern Town.* Greenhouse et al., *Law and Community in Three American Towns.*

43. Belk, *Making it Plain: Deconstructing the Politics of the American Prison-Industrial Complex.* Carlson, "Doing Good and Looking Bad: A Case Study of Prison/Community Relations." Thies, *The Big House in a Small Town: The Economic and Social Impacts of a Correctional Facility on its Host Community.* Gilmore, *Golden Gulag.*

Chapter Six

Cops and Corrections

Community policing is a policing strategy and philosophy based on the notion that community interaction and support can help control crime, with community members helping to identify suspects, and bring problems to the attention of police

William Skogan

Whether a town has been home to a prison for 100 years or for only three, there seems to be one overarching fear—the fear of escapes. It just comes with the fences, walls, and razor wire, I suppose. It is an often-discussed subject, although people make themselves feel better by assuming that any escaping inmate would be stupid to stay in a town where there are so many corrections officers (COs). I heard rumors that people left their keys in their cars so that any escapee could steal it without having to come into the house and endanger the residents. I found no real proof of this (although I did not go around pulling on car doors), but the stories alone showed me how important this issue was to the citizens of the towns that I was studying.

I spent nearly two years in two communities without ever hearing the siren that I had heard so much about. I was beginning to think that it was such a rarity that it really was nothing to fear. This was until a night in March when I first experienced a prison town after a breakout. At about 3:00 P.M., the inmate had simply walked away from his job at the prison dairy at a minimum-security institution. He was found to be missing at the 4:00 P.M. count when Department of Corrections (DOC) officials were sent out on search teams and local law enforcement was notified.

I spent numerous hours talking to prison and local officials about the relationship between these two seemingly autonomous entities thrust together through economic and political necessity. I sat in on meetings, talked to members of the community, and generally made a nuisance of myself prying in these people's lives. But it was not until I experienced the response to a prison escape that I saw how this relationship really worked.

The prison escape captures the imagination of the public as much as almost any facet of prison life. Stories of prison escapes become legendary, and I sat in on several conversations in which sheriffs and prosecutors would swap escape stories. (My favorite was about the inmate who left a monopoly card on his pillow after he escaped. It said, "Get out of jail free.") Ensuring that the stories do not become tragic depends on a solid working relationship between the prison and the local law enforcement. On this night, these groups seemed to have just that. As I drove around town, there were police cars from the surrounding towns as well as prison vans driving up and down the streets.

When I drove by the prison's property that evening, I saw prison personnel and local law enforcement on four wheelers with searchlights. The local stores all had the mug shot and description of the escapee. The entire area was blanketed. At 11:45 p.m., the man was caught near the county airport without incident. He had barely made it off of prison property. He has since been transferred to a more secure facility and will likely have five years added to his sentence.

This type of close working relationship does not just emerge; it takes a lot of effort. This relationship is more complicated than the one a town would normally have with its largest employer. It seems doubtful that IBM asks to borrow the town of Poughkeepsie's drug dogs or use its riot gear when employees get out of hand, but prison towns do get these types of calls from the institutions in their midst. The new prison town has to handle these and other issues, and the relationship between the prison and the local law enforcement determines how smoothly incidents like the one described above are worked out. Law enforcement and the prison administration have contact regarding various issues, and although a prison administrator might be fine without getting along with the town's politicians, life is more difficult when they do not play well with the local cops. I argue that how well this works is dependent on the level of government running the facility. The state prisons in my study are much more responsive to police concerns than the Federal Bureau of Prisons (BOP) and seem to place a greater emphasis on this responsiveness.

Given this, viewing the relationship from the standpoint of the local police is significant, not only because of what it tells us about the specific issue of community/prison relations, but also what it tells us more generally given the trend in police departments nationally toward a more community-based policing model. It has been argued that this model and its corollary "problem-oriented policing" have always been the foundation of any rural police force, even before there was a concept of "community policing" per se.[1] Community policing is based on a model in which officers and administrators are knowledgeable and responsive to those they are empowered to "protect and serve."[2] Rural policing has always had a strong focus on the "service" aspect of the job, with local cops acting in a much broader way than most urban police forces.[3] For this to work properly, the rural police need to have strong ties not only to the individuals on their "beat," but also with local community groups.

If one allows for the notion that the prison is one such community group, the way the prison interacts with the local police is an appealing way to look at one aspect of community policing.[4] For community-based policing to work in a rural area, the community needs to be responsive to the police as much as the police need to respond to the community. In other words, there are two distinct institutional actors that make community policing work: the police themselves and community actors/institutions. When a new community actor or group is added to the already existing makeup of the town, a test case in the effectiveness of community policing is created. In the prison town, the prison becomes one such community institution. The police may want to work with the prison, as seems to be the case for both towns in this study, but the responsiveness of the prison to this offer determines whether or not this is possible.

The two towns in my study show what several scholars have pointed out as one of the important parts in evaluating community policing—the responsiveness of the community being served.[5] We have two similarly situated institutions, the rural police of Beeville and Florence who are engaging in their own form of community policing. There is then the addition of several prisons to each community, in Beeville from the state and in Florence from the federal government. Whereas one might hypothesize that we would see a similar interaction, because a prison is a prison, this is not what takes place. Like the issues discussed from the other institutional standpoints, this is a question of political responsiveness and federalism.

The state institutions are more open to the local police force and become another community actor involved in community policing. This is not the case with the federal institutions.

The relationship between the courts and prisons is more complicated. Despite the regularity of the contact, the relationship is often more difficult than that with law enforcement. Inmates get involved in the court system in criminal and civil matters, and the effects of a new prison on the local court system can be extensive. When inmates commit crimes inside of the institution, they become the jurisdiction of the local courts. Because of this, many states have created special prosecutors to deal with crimes that occur inside of the prison, and states often promise to reimburse the local courts to help defray the costs of prosecution.[6] Even so, local courts are overwhelmed with these cases. For example, the Bee County district court has added another judge since the prisons have opened, although the population in the area has remained relatively stable.

As discussed by George Cole, the notion that the criminal justice system is, in fact, a system is but a myth. This is rarely more obvious than when all three are interacting in the same community. Relationships between the prison and the local government are forged, but the relationship with the local cops and courts are necessary, especially from a state institution. Much of the interaction between courts and prisons runs through the police department or sheriff's department. Although the prison does much in terms of transportation to the courts, for the most part, the two entities have little personal interaction. Whether a state or federal facility, there is little in the way of a developing relationship, although the impact a new prison has on the court system is enormous.

This chapter focuses on the relationship between community and prison from the viewpoint of the police and the courts. First, I will outline the current state of the literature on community policing, including studies of urban and rural areas. I will then argue that although the state facilities are conducive to a continuation of the community-policing style already in evidence, the federal facilities in my study are not. This evidence begins to show that, at least in this arena, the state government is more responsive to local concerns than the federal government. I will further argue that the evidence shows the importance of having a willing partner in the effort toward problem-oriented policing. I will then discuss the impact a new prison has on the local court system.

POLICE BEHAVIOR AND STRATEGIES

Studies of the police and police behavior have followed in much the same vein as that of prisons. Large studies of the organization were the norm until the mid-1970s, when research began to be narrowed to deal with specific aspects of police behavior.[7] These early works tried to understand the police on an organizational level, be it a whole department, as in Joel Skolnick's case, or individual police personnel within the department, as in the case of James Q. Wilson.

The second wave of police research was, in many ways, much like the "What works?" era of prison studies. They were proscriptive and policy-oriented in nature, trying to discern from empirical work what the most effective methods were to "fight crime." This was, as much as anything, a response to funding opportunities that grew out of the Nixon era's "War on Crime" and much like Willie Sutton's reasoning for robbing banks—scholars went where the money was. As Skogan and Frydl point out in their large-scale review of the state of the literature on the police, the studies born of this age ignored Skolnick and Wilson's focus on organizational behavior and shifted to focus on police patrols exclusively as if that were the main point of police functions.[8]

Many of these empirical studies of police behavior focused on the effects of police patrols on crime.[9] As such, they are much like the studies of rehabilitation efforts in prisons with their narrow and prescriptive nature and tell us little as a whole about police behavior on an organizational level. This would change in the 1980s with the rise of community-policing efforts and the studies of those efforts.[10] These studies were still very much prescriptive, but they looked at police behavior as part of a larger whole rather than an island of patrol units for which the only function was to "fight crime." These studies also focused on large urban areas (e.g., Houston, Newark, and Baltimore), and the findings are difficult to discern.

Part of the problem is definitional. Community policing seems to be an amorphous notion that even experts admit is hard to define. "In a definitional sense, community policing is not something one can easily characterize. . . . It assumes a commitment to broadly focused, problem-oriented policing and requires that police be responsive to citizens' demands when they decide what local problems are and set their priorities."[11] What exactly constitutes a community-policing effort is as difficult to pin down as the definition.[12] Programs such as the "broken windows" approach of New York City during the Giuliani administration, Chicago's notion of greater linkages between city agencies and the police departments under Mayor Daly, or Seattle's use of the federal "weed and seed" program to fight drug crime all fall under the larger umbrella of community policing.[13] A recent survey found that more than 90 percent of all cities larger than 250,000 people were engaging in some form of what they termed community policing and more than 85 percent of those departments had at least one full-time officer assigned as a specialist in the field.[14]

The success or failure of community policing is also difficult to gauge. In evaluating such programs, there are problems that arise from disparate factors from defining the community that is being served to what the appropriate "end" should be used as an appropriate measure. Do these measures seek to lower crime rates or just lower fear of crime? Are they just a way to view the police as a political institution that needs to be responsive to its constituency? Is better communication between institutional actors enough? All of these are potential goals of community policing, and as such, the evidence of these programs' success or failure seems to be mixed depending on the measures used and the individual definitions of community policing. For example, Wesley Skogan's study of Chicago, *Police and Community in Chicago: A Tale of Three Cities*, finds three very different experiences with community policing in Chicago depending on the racial makeup of the neighborhood.[15] William Lyons discusses what he terms the "competing stories" of community policing in Seattle, a city often considered a model case for the successes of such undertakings.[16] Lyons argues that such a statement is dependent on who within the power structure is defining this success—the police or the community being served—with the police arguing for the success of their programs and community groups having mixed feelings about these claims.

Problem-oriented policing places a great deal of importance on responsiveness to the community's concerns, and this is much more easily done in rural areas with smaller departments, yet these areas are mostly ignored by scholars. Ralph Weisheit, Edward Wells, and David Falcone argue that, in many ways, rural police departments are the perfect laboratories to see community policing at work.[17] The notions that community policing holds dear—citizen interaction, citizen feedback, and cops who intimately know their beat—are all part of the fabric of policing in small towns. But such studies are rare because scholars argue that studying rural police departments is a difficult proposition because of an inherent fear of outsiders in small towns, small sample size, and a feeling that rural police do not really do "police work" in the classic sense.[18]

Despite these problems, a few studies have been undertaken. These find that rural police do, in fact, focus on community policing to a large extent and are largely successful in their efforts.[19] In rural areas, police focus on crime prevention and service activities and were expected to perform a much wider range of functions than were their urban counterparts. Given the more close-knit nature of rural policing, police utilized a style that was more responsive to the citizenry than was seen in more urban areas. Most importantly, the community itself was responsive to the police's efforts in a much more comprehensive way than in urban areas.

These findings outline why notions of community policing matter to this study. Beyond the argument that rural police are inherently good laboratories in which to generally study community policing, the addition of a prison as a member of the community brings in an added element. As stated above, having a responsive community is vital for problem-oriented policing to work. As we will see, despite consistent attempts from the local police force to reach out to the federal prisons, little has been accomplished, and the only relationship that has evolved is one of mistrust and antagonism. This is not the case with the state prisons, in which the strong informal relationship has proven to have much more interaction, with positive and negative results.

POLICING IN RURAL PRISON TOWNS

Over the last 20 years, major urban centers have struggled to formulate some plan for integration of more community-based policing. Although Wesley Skogan found that many officers complained about performing what they deemed as "social work" functions,[20] several scholars have argued that it is just these kinds of activities that are routinely handled by rural cops. As Payne et al. put it ". . . police in small town were expected to fill several roles simultaneously. Moreover, small-town police officers were often called upon to assist in fixing personal problems that were beyond the scope of traditional law enforcement."[21] Although most scholars seem to consider community policing as inherently positive, the prison example shows some potential problems that will be discussed below. These problems may well be because they are on the same side of the power structure, a function of the classic "blue line" being extended to include those who wear the CO's uniform. This does not diminish the prison's role as a community organization as it pertains to the relationship with the police. This section outlines the "successful" community-policing effort between the police and the prison when a state facility is at issue and outlines the cracks in that system. It will also discuss the "failed" model with a federal facility.

The addition of a prison to a community seems to shake up the traditional role of a rural police force—what Payne, Berg, and Sun labeled "dogs, drunks, disorder, and dysfunction."[22] Although the addition of a prison may add to at least three of those functions (I'm not sure of any evidence that prison workers have more dogs than the general population), it also adds to the function of police in other areas. The first and most obvious example is with help in terms of aiding with escapes. Although escapes from any facility are rare, making sure that procedures are in place is necessary to protect the public. Another example has to do with the investigation of crimes occurring inside of a facility. Local police have weapons at their disposal such as access to drug-sniffing dogs and forensic teams that prisons lack. Local law enforcement can also help with the almost constant stream of inmates needing to go to local criminal and civil court.

According to Doug Dretke, former head of the Institutions Division for the Texas Department of Criminal Justice (TDCJ), a call to the local sheriff is going to be one of the first a new warden makes in Texas. From the perspective of the warden, regardless of type, this is an important relationship to facilitate. This is for practical rather than public relations reasons. The first reason was discussed already—the help needed when an inmate escapes. The ability of the prison to chase the inmate is limited, especially once they leave the property. Texas facilities have their own chase dogs, but not the manpower to send out. It is the sheriff's department who will begin to search for the inmate outside of the prison walls.

The second reason for contacting the sheriff is because of the sheer number of papers that are served on the inmates in a facility. Everything from divorce papers to bench warrants are served through the local sheriff's office, and Dretke estimates that someone from that office must come to a facility every day. Whether or not the relationship goes much beyond this seems to have much to do with the type of warden involved.

In Beeville and Florence, the police departments and sheriff's offices reached out to the prisons when they first opened up. Common wisdom would dictate that the relationship between these two criminal justice institutions should be relatively smooth regardless of the type of institution, but that is not the case. They both model themselves as paramilitary organizations that serve the same master—the criminal justice system. In fact, in several states, COs are considered peace officers, although this is not the case with federal employees or employees of the TDCJ.

Bob Horn, former sheriff of Bee County, Texas, spent many mornings having coffee and "visiting" with the warden of the TDCJ's McConnell Unit. The local sheriff has few formal "police" functions within the prison itself because the TDCJ's Inspector General (IG)'s Office does most of the investigations of crimes that occur on the inside. Despite this fact, he estimates that he receives one to four letters weekly from inmates tipping him off to laws being broken inside of the various facilities in town. He passes these tips on directly to the IG's office. However, he does have a function because he is responsible for serving civil papers on inmates and transporting them to the local courts for appearances.

Horn claims that these two functions, although seemingly simple, can be quite difficult and need a lot of coordination. Serving civil papers (e.g., for divorces) can be quite sensitive, and Horn claims that he and the warden would discuss the possible reaction of the inmate over their morning coffee. They would also discuss the inmates being transported to court so that Horn could plan for any potential problems. The warden often offered additional transportation support if he felt it was necessary. This is the best side of how the state police relationship that has developed in Beeville works.

There is also a downside. When a CO is arrested in town, the sheriff and police chief told me that their first call is to the warden of the appropriate facility. They wanted to find out more about the suspect in question. Although they never told me outright, I got the feeling that preferential treatment was given to good employees that was not given to the problematic ones.[23] This kind of cozy, backroom relationship has obvious problems. How a person is treated after being arrested should, in a perfect world, have nothing to do with how they act at work.

This is where the community-policing model in these rural communities may hit the limit of its usefulness and where we see the "blue line" being extended to those who work for the prisons. This may be a case of their similar careers coming into play. If IBM were the biggest employer in town, the Police might extend courtesies for the sake of community peace, but they seem to go even farther when dealing with prison employees. Despite being a community actor, the prisons seem to be a special community actor, one that gets even more consideration in the community-policing model in these rural towns. But their employees do get into trouble locally, and the police have a lot of interaction with COs when they are off duty.

Sheriff Bob Horn had many dealings with COs and their problems. The Capehart section of Bee County is former naval housing that has become affordable apartments where many COs choose to live. This neighborhood is outside of the city limits and is therefore in the sheriff's jurisdiction. In a town where the train tracks quite literally split the old Anglo and Latino sections of town, Capehart is a bit of an anomaly. It is the only truly ethnically diverse neighborhood in the county. This diversity is ethnic only, not socioeconomic. The cookie-cutter apartments and small houses that the military built have seen better days. Capehart is the "high crime" area that is in the sheriff's jurisdiction, and many of these problems are caused by COs. The Sheriff's Department does not keep statistics on what percentage of calls to Capehart are in response to problems with COs, but the deputies claim that many of the problems there involve the COs or their families.

The local police chief in Beeville has less interaction with the wardens than the sheriff because the prisons themselves are not inside of the city limits, but he has a similar coziness with the TDCJ as the sheriff's office (which also has the same inherent problems). Most of his direct interaction is more related to inmates who need to be sent to the local hospital. He sends out the SWAT team for such inmates, although he does not always think this is necessary. He claims it is more to make the citizenry comfortable than any real threat. This is community policing at work. A problem, whether real or perceived, is identified, and community actors and the police work together for a solution. Reduction in the fear of crime is one of the goals of community policing, and this is a case in which that is the aim of a policy.

One does not hear the same stories in Florence. In fact, there is little interaction between the police and prison at all anymore. The local police claim to have made many attempts to reach out to the prison and its employees, but they never saw their efforts pay off.[24] The animosity is obvious, and in interviews one often hears the employees of the prisons described in very derogatory terms.[25] The federal prisons have not been a willing partner in this relationship, and we see a failure to implement the community-policing model when the community actor is unwilling to take part.

In Florence, issues have come up through the years that have been brought to the attention of prison officials, but according to police officials, these concerns have been all but ignored. As I stated before, I attended several community relations board meetings at the federal facilities in Florence, and the chief of police and sheriff's empty seats spoke volumes. Despite the near dog-and-pony-show nature of these meetings, they could potentially be a forum to discuss police concerns. The police seem to have given up hope that this potential could be a reality.

The local police in Florence have made some specific complaints in the decade since the prison opened that have not been addressed to their satisfaction. After fears from the community and complaints by the police, the BOP did agree to put a security fence around its minimum-security camp (even with the chain link fence, the facility could still be mistaken for a local school), but they refused to change its security responses to escapes from that facility. It is BOP policy not to chase its escapees from the camp, and they have been unwilling to notify the local police when such walkaways occur.[26] Other issues raised by the local police have also gone unheeded, and as a result, the local police only interact with the prisons when necessary.[27]

There is an upside to this chilliness. Because so few COs who work for the BOP choose to live in Florence, the police there do not have the same problems that are seen in Beeville. Most of their negative dealings with the COs come in the form of traffic violations, and although TDCJ employees may be receiving preferential treatment, BOP employees claim that they are unfairly targeted by the local police on their commute out of town.[28]

Unlike the BOP, the TDCJ takes its walkaways very seriously, and when an inmate walked away from a community-service squad a few years ago, the Sheriff's Office and Beeville police were notified, and the local police captured the inmate within hours. The local police chief sees the prisons as just another community institution that he interacts with on a regular basis, and one can see the community-policing model at work. The example above of the SWAT team at the hospital is such a case. Despite his feeling that it is probably overkill, the chief takes the prison's needs and community's fears into account when it comes to potential escapes from the hospital. The prison has also responded in kind by sending extra COs with inmates for their hospital stays.

For the community-policing model to work, the police need a willing partner in the community institutions it serves. Rural police are used to working in this way, whether they call it community policing or not, and with the prisons, they reached out so that they could better serve them. But in my study, we see two very different responses to this. The reasons behind the differing responsiveness between state and federal facilities are the focus of the following section.

RESPONSIVENESS

The section above outlines the successes and failures of the community-policing model in the two communities, but it does not answer the question of why the Beeville police have close interaction with the local prisons whereas the Florence police do not. Part of the answer can be gleaned from previous chapters because, like the other institutions in this study, the answer comes down to electoral and bureaucratic political responsiveness and federalism. But in some ways, the federal government does not need help from the local police to the extent that the state does. Crimes committed inside of a federal facility are prosecuted in federal courts, and U.S. Marshals are used for transportation rather than the local sheriff's department. Civil lawsuits filed against the federal prison are similarly dealt with in the federal district court in Pueblo, Colorado, without any additional help needed from the locals.

This is not true for the state. As we saw above, the state prison depends on the sheriff's office to provide various services, including crime investigations, security during court proceedings, and the service of various court papers. They also rely on the locals during escapes from the minimum-security institutions, whereas the BOP does not even chase these inmates. Although these issues may appear to be minor, they take a great deal of coordination and a working relationship between these institutions.

These two institutions seem to have the fewest barriers to overcome in their relationship. Both institutions in Beeville agreed that part of the closeness between the cops and corrections there was due to their similar careers. They are on opposite ends of the same system, but they are both in paramilitary organizations that deal with the same clientele. These factors give them a common language and common point of reference. The local cops in Beeville feel comfortable picking up the phone and bringing issues directly to the prison administrators.

Given this, one might assume that although the BOP does not need the locals as much, they might still have a solid relationship. From the police side of the story, it does not seem that this is so much of an issue of bureaucratization as it is about the attitude of the federal employees toward the local police and vice versa. Because one might assume an easy relationship, this may be where the aloofness and sense of superiority that comes from the federal employees come through the strongest. Some of the barriers between community residents and prison employees are understandable in that they live in very different worlds. Both cops and COs are notoriously cliquish and tend to insulate themselves from people outside of the fray.[29] I was told that in Beeville there is some cross-pollination in which COs and cops will become friendly off of the job. I never heard of such things in Florence. Instead I heard accusations of profiling by the local police and a general lack of communication between the two institutions. Over time, what was simply apathy has become more akin to animosity. This animosity and lack of communication seems like it will be difficult to overcome, if there is any interest in doing so.

Part of the difference in the responsiveness is for practical reasons. The state needs help from the local police that the federal government may not. One example is in emergency management. Beeville is near the Gulf of Mexico and has been part of hurricane evacuations in the past. To facilitate the evacuation of thousands of inmates, the state relies on the local sheriff and police for help. "The federal government has planes that they can fly in for help," Doug Dretke tells me, "but we need a lot of help from the community in an emergency."

That help may come in strange ways. When inmates overpowered a CO in the administrative segregation cell block in the McConnell Unit in December 1999, 80 inmates got out of their cells and took over the block. The uprising never got out of the pod, and inmates were returned to their cells in four hours. Warden Prasifka notified the local police and sheriff about the problem and within the hour, the police, including off-duty officers, had surrounded the perimeter of the facility. Fortunately they were not needed, but their help was welcomed just the same.

The TDCJ has been known to return the favor. The TDCJ's offices at the former naval air station have been used on several occasions as staging areas for hurricane relief. The department offered the use of their transportation division to evacuate local residents despite their own concern that they would have to move some 7,000 inmates out of the area. The closeness and good working relationship that has developed over time has led to the give and take we can see. Dretke argues that time is a vital factor involved in the closeness between these groups: "In Beeville, a new Warden at the McConnell Unit is still front-page news. The community has a higher level of ownership in the unit because they worked so hard to get it. The same isn't true in a place like Huntsville."

Dretke claims that in Huntsville, the sheer number of units (eight) and the length of time there have been prisons makes a new warden fairly unimportant. That may be partially true, but Huntsville is more urban than Beeville, located just 60 miles from the fourth-largest city in the country—Houston. It is also larger than Beeville and is dependent on two industries instead of just one. Huntsville is also home to Sam Houston State University, a school of nearly 20,000 students. For a rural community, even one that has been home to a prison a long time, this might still be true.[30]

Although the prisons in Beeville have been opened for over a decade, Ernie Gutierrez, the current warden at the McConnell Unit, has many meetings with local politicians and police. The meetings with the local police and sheriff are especially important. But Gutierrez only has to water the seeds that were planted by previous wardens like Prasifka. It makes for a much easier row to hoe, to continue the metaphor. If the prison and town have developed the kind of relationship we see in Beeville, it can only help when an eventual problem, like an escape or a staff murder, takes place. The relationships with the local courts need the same kind of care afforded to the relationship with local law enforcement. After the police, the courts have the most day-to-day interaction with the facility in civil and criminal matters.

COURTS

Texas Special Prosecutor Herb Hancock and Karnes County Sheriff David Jalufka were sitting and having coffee before a grand jury hearing in February 2003. Hancock works for a group that specifically prosecutes state inmates for crimes committed inside of the facilities. The conversation moved to a discussion of escapes, specifically the so-called "Texas Seven" who escaped from the maximum-security unit in town in December 2001. This escape led to a shootout in the parking lot at the local Wal-Mart; the death of a police officer in Irving, Texas; the suicide of one of the inmates; and the eventual capture in Woodland Park, Colorado, of the others. The six captured inmates were all sentenced to death. I asked Hancock and Jalufka why they think this escape took place so soon after the facility was opened. Both men agree: flushing the toilet.

"Flushing the toilet" is what prison officials call the assumption that wardens send their most difficult inmates to the newest prison in the correctional system. Although one would think that dangerous inmates, such as the men described above, would be the most likely to be flushed, local prosecutors and judges said that it was the so-called "writ-writers" who the wardens were most eager to get rid of. A "writ-writer" is an inmate who sues the prison system for various civil rights violations by the facility. These civil cases flood the courts, and as one local judge in a new prison town said, "you have to look at all of them, because you never know which of these are real and which are frivolous."[31]

Much has been written on inmate litigiousness as compared to the general population.[32] These studies have found that although inmates are more litigious in terms of the sheer number of cases, when one looks deeper into the issue, it is not so simple. Eisenburg argues that looking at inmate filings without looking at opportunities for filings and their eventual success rates only tells part of the story.[33] He finds that inmates are not much more litigious than most citizens, but they have many more opportunities to file suits because their civil rights are infringed upon much more often than the average person.

Despite this research, the assumption that inmates were clogging up courts led to the passage of the Prison Litigation Reform Act of 1996 (PLRA), originally a part of Newt Gingrich's "Contract with America," which attempted to give judges more leeway to dismiss suits and generally make it more difficult for inmates to bring such litigation in the first place. Inmate filings accounted for nearly 20 percent of the federal court's docket before the passage of the PLRA, and the legislation attempted to change that. The PLRA essentially tries to streamline the inmate litigation process, limits inmates' access to courts for so-called frivolous suits, and makes it more difficult for inmates who consistently lose lawsuits to get *in forma pauperis* status.[34]

Judge Joel Johnson of the Texas 156th Judicial District, of which Beeville is a part, argues that the changes made by the PLRA, especially the section that allows him to hold hearings on closed-circuit television, have helped move cases through. Margo Schlanger finds that overall, inmate filings are down after the passage of the PLRA.[35] Despite this, even in the post-PLRA era, the burden of a new prison on the courts system is extensive. My research shows that a new facility brings an average of nearly 40 inmate civil filings in federal district court that are related to the conditions by the second year a facility is opened.[36]

These so-called 1983 filings by inmates, named for the section of the United States Civil Code they are filed under, are going to be a large part of a federal docket. A new prison means that a federal judge will not have experience in dealing with inmate lawsuits that will eventually become a large part of his or her docket. For example, for the period of September 1, 2008, to September 1, 2009, Federal District Judge Janis Jack of the Southern District of Texas's court in Corpus Christi had 1,337 filings related to prisoner issues. This represented 21.5 percent of her total docket: 438 of those filings were 1983 filings, 7 percent of the total filings in her court. Although some of these filings may have merit, many do not. "The courts just assumed that every inmate was telling the truth all of the time at the beginning. They did not realize that inmates will sometimes lie or that uses of force are only used when an inmate refuses to comply with orders," former Warden Prasifka says.

A citizen warden can help smooth the way. Tommy Prasifka was having problems with such lawsuits even after the McConnell Unit had been open for a while. The other wardens had little luck with Judge Jack. According to Prasifka, a new judge may not understand the nature of many inmate lawsuits and will hold hearings on every filing. This means transporting inmates to court and pulling staff out of the institution to testify. After testifying in several trials, Prasifka invited Judge Jack to visit the unit. He offered to show her anything she wanted to see. After touring several parts of the prison, the judge turned to Prasifka and said that she had seen enough. According to Prasifka, she pointed out that an inmate could do his time without any problems with the COs if he chose to. Unless he acted up, the COs would leave him alone.

Prasifka said that things were much easier after that. He would still be called to testify on occasion, and the TDCJ still lost its share of cases, but he felt as if the judge had a better idea of what she was dealing with. She was more likely to take an inmate's word with a grain of salt. Prisoner's rights advocates might find this problematic, but from the TDCJ's perspective, this is just good public relations for the department. This is also what a citizen warden should do. This is about education, in this case of a federal judge, about the inner working of a closed world. Getting a realistic view of what is going on the inside of the razor wire can only help.

There are not as many inmate suits going into the state courts, but there are still many tort suits that need to be dealt with. It is with these civil suits, more so than the criminal proceedings, that the court system becomes taxed. A rural small-town judge would have little or no experience in dealing with inmate lawsuits.

On the criminal side, prison prosecutors have a difficult job under the best of circumstances because their conviction rates are much lower than those of regular district attorneys.[37] One prosecutor told me that "most people think that these problems should be dealt with internally" and that "getting convictions is very tough."[38] For example, many states have problems with COs getting "gassed" or "chunked" as it is called. This is when an inmate sprays urine and feces at a CO when he or she is walking by. Several states, including Texas, can prosecute this activity as assault, but prosecutors told me that they have a difficult time getting convictions on these charges because "local residents just kind of think it's the cost of doing business" for a CO.[39] When I sat in on grand jury indictments, the prosecutor took great pains to explain why indicting on these charges was so important, something he said that regular prosecutors rarely have to do. Senior prison officials have great discretion as to what types of crimes are dealt with internally and what they send out, and overloading the prosecutor with weak charges that may be better off in administrative rather than legal proceedings can cause problems. Additionally, these are the kinds of problems that prison officials would rather keep off the local community's radar screen, if possible.

When it comes to new prisons, there are two other concerns as they pertain to courts. The first is about security when bringing inmates to court. Rural county courthouses are built for looks rather than security, and ensuring that an inmate does not escape is of primary concern. David Davidson, a former captain with the TDCJ's Transport Department, described how some courts had no holding cells and had many points through which an inmate could escape. One time, two inmates were awaiting trial at a rural courthouse in Texas that did not have accommodations for holding prisoners. The judge told the transportation officers to keep the inmates in a converted closet that was sometimes used as a jury room. Two unarmed transport officers were inside of the room with the inmates while armed guards waited outside. One of the officers got curious about boxes that were being housed against the back wall. He opened one and was shocked to see a half a dozen guns in the box, evidence from a trial held years before. He moved the inmates back to the transport van and informed the judge. The judge had forgotten that they were in there.

This story exemplifies the importance of good communication and relationship building. According to Davidson, it starts by talking to the bailiff and then the judge. Over time, the supervisors must develop relationships with the judge to ensure that security is not breached. This is just as important during a jury trial. When standing trial, inmates are put in civilian clothes and sit in the courtroom unrestrained. Most judges require that the TDCJ officers keep enough distance so that a jury is not prejudiced against the defendant because prior bad acts or the fact that an inmate is incarcerated is often excluded from evidence. The defendant must also be able to have confidential communications with his or her attorney. Often attorneys will want to take their clients to a separate room to discuss the defense. Officers find this problematic, and compromises must be reached. If the transportation officer has a good relationship with the judge, security can be ensured while a fair trial takes place.

Davidson says that the most dangerous time during a trial is at verdict and sentencing. The inmate will sometimes be overcome with emotion or assume this is his best chance to escape. The TDCJ has to ensure that the inmate stays safe and secure, and working with the local police can help reduce the likelihood of any trouble. Davidson said that he placed supervisors in certain areas because of long-standing relationships. There are six transport hubs and supervisors who are from a specific area to smooth things over. "The first thing I would tell a new supervisor is to go and talk to the bailiff and the judge. I always tried to pick people who were already known in town and might be known. This helps ensure that a judge will listen to us," Davidson says.

This is further evidence of the importance of relationship building. Understanding how a rural community works and the importance of personal relationships helps smooth the way. However, with courts, the federal facilities have a distinct advantage and a lesser need to work issues out. All matters that pertain to the prison run through the federal courts, and the dealings are with federal employees. Most federal district courts are located in larger urban areas nearby, allowing the BOP to bypass the local court structure and its security problems.

CONCLUSIONS

So why are there problems with the federal facility in Florence that do not exist with the state facility in Beeville? The two groups must interact on certain issues, so where does the animus with the federal facility come from? Why is it that Beeville's police and sheriff seem to work so closely together with the prisons, whereas the Florence police, although willing, never have? The answer to these questions seems to show the importance of having a willing partner in any community-policing effort. The police in both communities reached out to this new constituency to try to bring them into the fold, but with very different results.

Both communities have had a remarkable amount of stability in their respective heads of the police departments and sheriff's departments since the prisons have opened, but in the past year, the local chief of police in Florence and the county sheriff in Beeville have retired. Whether or not there is a change in the relationships between the police and the prisons with this change will not be evident for some time. In a brief phone interview, the new chief of the Florence police stated that reaching out to the prisons is something he is planning on doing but has not done yet. If the past is an indicator of future behavior on their part, the prisons in Florence are unlikely to respond with much enthusiasm.

NOTES

1. Falcone et al., "The Small-Town Police Department." Weisheit et al., "Community Policing in Small Town and Rural America." Payne, Berg, and Sun, "Policing in Small Town America: Dogs, Drunks, Disorder, and Dysfunction."

2. Skogan et al., *Community Policing: Chicago Style*. Lyons, *The Politics of Community Policing: Rearranging the Power to Punish*. Skogan, *Police and Community in Chicago: A Tale of Three Cities*.

3. Weisheit et al., *Crime and Policing in Rural and Small Town America*.

4. Lyons, Skogan, and others who study community policing spend a great deal of time discussing community organizations, institutions, and activists, so stretching the definition of the community to be dealt with to the prison as an institution hardly seems out of order.

5. One of the major problems scholars have found with community policing is that police forces are slow to change or unwilling to do so at all (Lyons, *The Politics of Community Policing: Rearranging the Power to Punish*). This is not the case in rural communities where police are already involved in many of the activities that proponents of community policing cherish.

6. Personal communication with Gina DeBotis, March 2004.

7. Wilson, *The Variety of Police Behavior: The Management of Law and Order in Eight Communities*.

8. Frydell and Skogan, *Fairness and Effectiveness in Policing: The Evidence*.

9. Kelling, "Police Field Services and Crime: The Presumed Effects of a Capacity."

10. Wilson and Kelling, "Broken Windows." Skogan, *Community Policing.*

11. Skogan et al., *Community Policing: Chicago Style*, 5.

12. The definitional problem runs deeper as well. Just the term "community" is rife with problems, depending on who a scholar considers to be a part of the community. For my purposes, I use the term community in the broadest sense possible, including all institutional actors within a geographic area.

13. Skogan et al., *Community Policing: Chicago Style*. Miller, *The Politics of Community Crime Prevention: Implementing Weed and Seed in Seattle*. Lyons, *The Politics of Community Policing: Rearranging the Power to Punish*.

14. http://www.policyarchive.org/handle/10207/bitstreams/874.pdf.

15. Skogan, *Police and Community in Chicago: A Tale of Three Cities*.

16. Lyons, *The Politics of Community Policing*.

17. Weisheit et al., "Community Policing in Small Town and Rural America."

18. Payne et al., 31–32.

19. Weisheit, *Studying Drugs in Rural Areas: Notes from the Field*. O'Shea, "Community Policing in Small Town Rural America," 59–76.

20. Skogan, *Police and Community in Chicago: A Tale of Three Cities*.

21. Payne et al., "Policing in Small Town America: Dogs, Drunks, Disorder, and Dysfunction," 38.

22. Payne et al., "Policing in Small Town America: Dogs, Drunks, Disorder, and Dysfunction."

23. I found what might have been one major exception. In one case, a high-ranking uniformed officer got into some problems of which he was later acquitted. At the time of his arrest, the warden was one who had a very difficult relationship with the town, and there had been an incident between a group of prison trainees and some deputy sheriffs. The officer was convinced that the arrest and subsequent trials (the first ended in a hung jury) were payback for the incident, a reprisal against the prison system. It was difficult to discern whether this was an example of the citizen/hermit dichotomy, because the warden at the time certainly fit the hermit mold, or if the officer in question was a "problem child." I was strongly advised not to speak to him by several people, and when I did finally interview him, he told me that his career has been seriously hurt by the incident.

24. I want to be clear that this is the police's side of the story. The BOP officials I talked to dodged any effort made to get them to talk in specifics about the local police, except to mention the profiling charges against the police discussed below.

25. Local police officers in Florence asked not to be quoted directly; therefore, this section is more observational than interview-based. When interview data are used, I summarize and paraphrase.

26. Just to be clear, the camp houses the lowest-security inmates with fewer than six months left in their sentences. These camps are what have come to be known colloquially as "club fed," a term that came from the seemingly lush conditions and a federal prison camp in northern Pennsylvania that shared a driveway with the local country club.

27. I am not being evasive as to the other "issues" involved, but I agreed not to put them in this study during an interview.

28. This may well be a backward way of getting some economic benefit from the prison because the biggest effect seems to be on those services catering to commuter traffic.

29. Fleischer, *Warehousing Violence*. Skogan, *Police and Community in Chicago: A Tale of Three Cities*. Several COs explained to me the difficulty they had maintaining friendships outside of other officers. They argued that it was difficult to explain to people what they did and what they had to deal with at work. It would seem that there would be a problem trying to explain to the average citizen that your job includes such issues as having fermented urine and feces thrown at you or having a 300-pound muscle-bound inmate come after you with a homemade knife.

30. In fact, I saw evidence of this while doing research in Florence. Next-door Cañon City has been home to a prison since 1871 and currently has nine state facilities. The wardens of these facilities are often in the news, perhaps because the prisons are the main industry in town.

31. Personal communication, February 2004.

32. Schlanger, "Inmate Litigation."

33. *Ibid.*

34. Essentially, the PLRA attempts to streamline the inmate litigation process, limit inmates' access to courts for so-called "frivolous suits," and make it more difficult for inmates who consistently lose lawsuits to get *in forma pauperis* status.

35. Schlanger, "Inmate Litigation."

36. Williams et al., "Courts and Corrections: The Effect of Prisons on Local and Federal Courts." Paper presented at the Law and Society Annual Conference, May 2008.

37. Personal communication, HH, January 2004.

38. *Ibid.*

39. *Ibid.*

Chapter Seven

Conclusion

In May 2009, House Republicans proposed the Keep Terrorists Out of America Act. President Obama was proposing to close the Guantanamo Bay detention center, but he did not want to simply free the detainees. He was proposing moving them to a facility in the United States, perhaps by expanding ADX Florence, which already had experience in housing inmates such as Ramsey Yussef and Richard Reid. There was also a discussion of moving the detainees to some new facility, as yet determined.

Although the Republicans were using this moment to try to wind up the American public, rural communities were already lobbying for the right to house the detainees. Communities in Montana, Tennessee, and Illinois, just to name a few, made pitches to the federal government to have the new facility located in their town. In December 2009, the government decided to purchase a half-filled facility in Thomson, Illinois, and retrofit the facility for the Department of Defense's needs. The administration estimates the creation of 3,800 jobs in and around Thomson.

Urban and suburban Americans seemed surprised by the rural communities. John Boehner and the Republicans, who depend on the rural vote, must have been even more surprised. I was not.[1] It has been two decades since the TDCJ has had to convince a town to allow a prison in their midst, and many rural American towns have become more concerned with jobs than escaped convicts.

What we have seen in the preceding chapters is, in many ways, about the broad consequences and realities of a simple choice—the choice to use prisons as an economic development strategy. Despite this simplicity, the difficulties that have emerged have little or nothing to do with the original policy choice. The desperation that led to this path is palpable to anyone who visits either community, even nearly two decades after the lobbying process began. The ramifications of this choice continue to be felt today.

Deciding whether or not these prisons have been a "success" in an economic sense seems to be beside the point. The prisons dotting our rural landscape are a reality whether they are having the hoped-for economic effects or not. It is highly unlikely that many of them, if any of them, will close anytime in the near future. Given this, there is a need to have a better understanding of what we now have and what the future holds for hundreds of rural communities.

Policy arguments in Washington and state capitals about the prison-building boom are an important part of this discussion, whether one sees a prison-industrial complex as a reality or not. The prison population boom has leveled off in the last few years, but states still have yet to "catch up" to the boom of the 1980s and 1990s. Even California, whose powerful corrections officers' union has fought hard to keep privatization out of the state system, has proposals to send inmates to prison facilities in other states to ease overcrowding. This is in addition to the current $7.8 billion plan to build new facilities to ease a prison system running at nearly 175 percent capacity. The plan failed, and a federal judge has ordered California to release 46,000 inmates. The state has appealed that decision, and the U.S. Supreme Court has agreed to hear the appeal in the 2010–2011 term.[2] If the plan had been successful, these new prisons were likely to go to rural communities that are lining up for them. Although the numbers do not seem to show that the prison will really help them, towns are still eager to land a facility, and, as the former Director of Institutions for the Texas Department of Criminal Justice (TDCJ) told me, the state will not even consider going to a community that does not want them. They do not have to anymore.

Rural prisons all over the United States are now a fact, and policy discussions about whether this is a good or bad thing are somewhat superfluous. We need to move beyond this and try to understand what happens when the lobbying process is but a faint memory and the new prison is no longer so new. This chapter will discuss some of the major findings of this dissertation, with ideas of how to improve these problems in the future and some fruitful areas for future study.

At a core level, nearly every issue we have seen through this research has come about because of problems in communication. Problems of interinstitutional communication breakdowns are seen throughout, and these types of issues are going to be commonplace between any bureaucratic organizations. There are three areas where these concerns show themselves to the largest degree: promises and expectations not realized during the lobbying stage, communication between state or federal entities and the local government, and communication between the prison administrators and the community.

THE PROBLEMS OF THE PRISON DERBY

In chapter three, we saw how these two rural communities, with little in common other than poverty and economic hardship, both chose a path that they hoped would pull them out of their economic woes. This may or may not have happened in either case because there have been intervening factors that may have affected the hard economic data, but neither community got everything it expected from the prisons. The reason for this has to do with the lobbying process itself and the tendency of both sides to upsell to the other without looking beyond the surface sales pitches.

Jobs are the first and most obvious place where this occurs. The types of numbers discussed by both the Bureau of Prisons (BOP) and Texas Department of Corrections were unrealistic at best and ridiculous at worst, but neither community did its due diligence in determining how realistic the figures were. There are two issues at play here. The first has to do with the number of qualified potential employees in an area. The second, which is related to the first, has to do with the nature of the work itself and how few qualified applicants will even be able to be successful in the job.

The BOP's intensive screening process and its ability to discriminate based on age meant that very few local residents in Florence ever had a chance at the potential jobs in the first place. Although this was not as great of a problem in Beeville, the rigors of working in a maximum-security institution were, and with the addition of two new units, the labor pool quickly dried up. This meant that the prisons needed to bring employees in from the outside, and if the towns were to get any additional benefit, it would have to come from new people moving to the area.

These issues may not have been avoidable, but they were not unforeseen. In the few studies that have been done on the issue, none show that anything close to 60 percent of jobs go to local people, but that magic number is still used during the lobbying process. Because these towns are clamoring for their chance to get a prison facility, there seems to be no harm in having a more realistic approach to the lobbying process. It would be a fairly simple proposition for the state and the federal government to keep records of their hiring practices at new facilities and to find out how many of their employees actually live there after the facility is in place.[3]

On the other side of this issue, the communities themselves need to have good affordable housing available to prison employees as well as other important amenities such as access to a social life and ancillary jobs for spouses and partners. The housing issue solved itself in Beeville with the closing of the naval air station and the opening up of all of the housing there, but one must wonder if Beeville would have enjoyed as many employees moving to town without this affordable housing. It seems obvious to say that a town needs to have enough places for employees to live, but there was little or no discussion of these needs during the lobbying process in either town.

Having other amenities for prison employees is a problem that would be difficult to plan for. Towns desperate for prison jobs are, by their very nature, already running short on good jobs for people who already live there, much less those who might relocate to the area. Otherwise, they would not be lobbying for the prison in the first place. Also, offering an active social world for prison employees, outside of the requisite downtown bars, may not happen before the prison opens. Many employees seem to be willing to live elsewhere and commute to have these things, and this is a bigger problem if there is a larger city within easy commuting distance.

Overall, both sides in the prison derby need to fully assess the situation before the prison comes to town and use the current evidence of what issues will be problematic at the start. An environmental assessment, like the one done by the BOP before siting the prison in Florence, is a good step, but some sort of social environmental impact study may be just as appropriate. We are beginning to be more aware of issues of social justice, and there are many scholars studying these problems. Perhaps shining their scholarly light on potential new prison towns would be helpful in this regard. However, this will do little for the problems of responsiveness that crop up after the prison opens.

IT'S ALL ABOUT THE DISTANCE REDUX

A common theme in all of the substantive chapters is the difference in the relationship between the state institutions and the community and the federal government and the community. As was mentioned briefly in a footnote, this may be an interesting variation on the principal-agent theory that is often used in discussing bureaucratic responsiveness. It is an admittedly imperfect connection, because in the case of prisons, the state is the principal and the agent, as is the federal government with the BOP, but it does bring up interesting issues for consideration.

However, if one takes the principal-agent notion a step further, it may well be that the state and federal governments, through the TDCJ and the BOP, are the principals whereas the local prisons are the agents. If this is the case, it begs the question as to whether there is something about the agents that is different that has little to do with the state/federal dichotomy I have raised. This is a fruitful area for further research that will be discussed below because it may well be that there is something special about the culture of corrections in Texas, or even just in Beeville's prisons, that breeds the responsiveness seen in this study.

Although it may be true that there is something different about the way the TDCJ views its role in the community, from what I saw, there is little reason to assume that what was seen in Florence is not true elsewhere as well.[4] There was a difference culturally that is evident among the federal employees, and it is difficult to imagine that this does not exist systemwide given the frequency of transfers and promotions among institutions.

The transient nature of prison employees is also evident with the BOP. It almost seems as if the notion of making sure that inmates do not become too entrenched in any single facility (this practice is called "doing life on a bus") has been extended to the staff as well. It is understandable that one would want to move promoted personnel so that they do not have to supervise those with whom they once worked, but this practice does not aid the community. Ken Chesshir, the mayor of Beeville, discussed that "one-in-a-hundred" prison employee who truly lays down roots in the community, and although this means that there are few who do, at least there are some who do so. This does not seem to be the case in the federal system.

As I said previously, the goal of a prison system should never be community relations, but given the growing number of prison towns, this seems to be an aspect of prison management that could be improved in some circles. This would not be a difficult proposition. From my conversations with community leaders, the bar of expectations is actually quite low. An occasional appearance at community events and a few informal conversations about issues that come up could salve many wounds. It may well be, given the large bureaucratic entity that the BOP is a part of, that complaints made to the BOP will not make their way down to the prison, but if more wardens were willing to cut out the bureaucracy and reach out directly to the communities in which they serve, Washington could be avoided altogether.

Although I am certainly critical of the BOP in Florence, I have anecdotal evidence that there are small towns where they have done a better job with community relations. However, when this has happened, it seems that it was the individual warden who made it a priority. Unfortunately, this often occurs after a tragedy or scandal of some sort, like the "cowboy" scandal in Florence, in which Joe Gunja was brought in to smooth things over inside and outside of the facility. A similar situation occurred in Atwater, California, when corrections officer (CO) Jose Rivera was killed in June 2008. Hector Rios was brought in and improved relations while also making Atwater a safer prison for staff and inmates.[5]

CITIZENS AND HERMITS REDUX

The importance of the individual warden to the prison-community relations may be one of the most important in this study. The "citizen" warden can ease many of the tensions that will inevitably arise in the relationship. I want to make it clear that I am not arguing that community relations should be the focal point of any warden's job. A warden's primary mission is security related, and being a good public relations aficionado is not a vital part of the security apparatus. The job of a warden has changed over the past 30 years, and dealing with outside issues has become of growing importance. The community-relations part of the job is no different than the politicization that has taken place in other areas and in many ways takes even less effort. The community does not expect that wardens are going to make appearances at all community events, but simple things such as an occasional chamber of commerce function makes the community feel like they have a partner in the prisons.

These types of appearances, coupled with community-service projects by inmates, are not so taxing as to take away from a warden's day-to-day job functions. It also seems to be a learned behavior. The importance of being a good citizen should be stressed by the top officials to everyone working at a facility, but especially for those at the top. The knowledge of the importance of good community relations will be passed along from warden to major when that major works his way up the ladder. We saw how Warden Scott did this with then-Major Prasifka, who then did so with Major Fernandez when he became a warden. By reaching outward, the prison staff may be able to more effectively avoid some of the pitfalls that occur when there is a large influx of people descending on a small rural town.

Seminars, training sessions, and other classes now abound in the corrections world. Sam Houston State University in Huntsville, Texas, houses the Correctional Management Institute of Texas, which runs programs for corrections professionals, including their Warden Peer Interaction Program that I had the honor of attending in 2009. In this program, wardens from across the country get together to discuss issues in prison management. Programs like this could discuss the importance of community relations with the wardens who attend, and wardens might use workshop strategies to improve community relations and learn from each other.[6]

PRIVATE PRISONS

This study was focused on two towns—one with state facilities, the other federal. I did not spend time in a community that went the other way and welcomed a private prison corporation into their midst. The private prison industry has grown along with the building boom, and their successes and failures have been well documented.[7] What has not been discussed are the effects these types of prisons have on rural areas.

FUTURE RESEARCH

There are four areas of research that were not developed well enough and need to be given a more quantitative approach than has been the case here or just need a level of detail that I was not able to give. The first three are related to courts, jobs and housing, and prison labor. The fourth has to do with issues of race and rural prison towns. The fifth is a more general need for more research on this theme as a whole.

The first area where more research is needed has to do with courts. This study only afforded a general overview of the effect of new prisons on courts and this area needs further development. Although most prisoner lawsuits end up in federal courts eventually, state institutional civil suits do weave their way through the state court system. The federal government has the resources to deal with these cases much more effectively, whereas the states do not.[8] There is the additional influx of criminal cases to state courts, and despite Texas's attempts to alleviate some of this case pressure by having a separate group of prison prosecutors, the rest of the court system is still burdened with these inmates. A study of the effects of new prisons on courts throughout the country would begin to show how much these communities were overburdened with these cases.

The second area pertains to jobs and housing mentioned above. A study of hiring patterns and housing data for these new prison communities would tell us much more than the current studies of income levels and unemployment rates. These studies, although useful, cannot give us a realistic picture of what is really happening. The recent study by Hooks et al. gave us a good baseline to work with in comparing unemployment rates in prison counties versus nonprison counties during the past 50 years, but we need a better measure.[9] In both of the towns I studied, the rise and fall of unemployment rates can be explained by other reasons, and unemployment is only one measure through which to determine the economic "success" or "failure" of a prison. Determining how many prison jobs are going to local community members and how many prison employees call these small towns home is a more specific measure to determine what these towns are getting and what other towns can expect to get.

The third area for research has to do with prison labor generally and community-service squads specifically. Prison labor is an often-discussed topic that has rarely been studied in an empirical way by social scientists. There are works on the legal issues involved, papers on the concerns of local labor groups about prison labor, and corrections department claims of lower recidivism rates as well as their own cost-benefit analyses. Research that marries the theoretical concerns regarding prison labor with the empirical reality of it would be useful, especially when most states have severely cut back on their prison industries' programs and inmate idleness is high.

The community-service squads themselves are an interesting subgroup of prison labor. Although lawsuits abound by inmates who work inside of the prison, I found no such suits brought by inmates who work on the service squads, despite the difficulty of the jobs and the low pay, even by prison standards. I have found no evidence that scholars have looked into these squads and their costs and benefits. It may be that if these programs were greatly expanded, there would be similar complaints by local labor leaders in the same way that we hear complaints about prison industry jobs taking away jobs on the outside, but perhaps not. These inmates are working on projects for the government that otherwise might not be done at all.

Although this appears to be a program that might be greatly expanded upon, there are two potential problems with this. First, prison managers must be very selective in the inmates they choose to work on these projects. It is difficult to imagine anything more tragic than one of these inmates escaping or worse—escaping and committing a heinous crime. Additionally, the inmates currently working on these projects are volunteers, which probably explains the lack of lawsuits pertaining to the practice. Prison officials told me that there were many more people who wanted to get on these work crews than positions available, but this may not continue if the programs are expanded. Forcing inmates to do this work would be akin to the chain gangs of old (and new), which might take away from the goodwill that seems to develop when these inmates do the work.

The effects on race relations as a consequence of having a large prison facility in a rural community need a more detailed look. I was struck by how little the local communities thought about or were aware of this as a potential problem. A survey using implicit and explicit measures of racial attitudes that compares rural prison communities to similarly situated nonprison towns might shed some light on this problem. It was nearly impossible not to be struck by the sight of mainly African American inmates in stark white uniforms doing manual labor outside of the courthouse in Beeville or working the fields at the McConnell Unit. It had a slave-days feel to it and it unnerved me. How this sight might affect racial perceptions was not something that locals wanted to discuss with me. Whether this was because they were unaware of the problem or unwilling to delve into the issue, I do not know. A survey on the subject might help shed some light on the issue.

The fifth and most obvious are several variations on the themes developed in this research. Given the inherent and admitted flaws in my research design, a broader study of some of the overarching themes might be fruitful. There are several variations that might be appropriate. One would be to study more new prison towns, some with state institutions and some with federal ones, to determine if my arguments about political responsiveness exist outside of my the communities studied here.

More interesting may be a study that looks at community relations in old prison towns as opposed to new ones. One would be able to find out if some of the issues I have found work themselves out over time, and if so, how. It might also be that these problems become more entrenched and problematic with the passage of time, showing how important the early stages, especially the lobbying stage, are in the set up for the eventual relationship. The ability to look at communities that have housed prisons for many years might also be useful in showing the pitfalls that are still to come for the newer prison towns.

This broader work may also be able to expand my very simple dichotomy between the citizen and hermit wardens. There may indeed be many levels in between here, something akin to James Q. Wilson's eight styles of police behavior that can only be determined with a larger group of wardens to study or with a more specified interest in just the behavior of prison administrators as it pertains to community relations.

BROADER IMPLICATIONS

The current scholarship on prisons as a distinct institution seems to assume that despite the changes in the prison world, individual prisons are, to a great extent, still well within the Goffman notion of the total institution.[10] Viewing prisons through this lens leads to a focus on what goes on inside of the institution itself rather than interinstitutional relations. Whereas the other criminal justice institutions, especially the police, have often been studied in terms of their relationship to the outside world, prisons are not studied as such. They are treated in one of two ways. One views them as a policy choice, some nondistinct part of the prison-industrial complex. This focus leads to little interest in prisons themselves and instead focuses on the various groups and institutions that make criminal justice policy. The other way to look at them is as an island or grouping of islands. This method forgets, if you will excuse the metaphor, that these islands are surrounded by an ocean and have linkages to the mainland as well. For example, although the literature on individual police departments assumes an interaction with the community as a whole, individual prisons are rarely viewed in this light.

One cannot ignore the great amount of interaction individual prisons have with the world around them. This dissertation proposes looking at prisons through a new lens: not as a total institution that can be studied in a vacuum, but as a political and legal institution to be studied the same way that the courts and the police are. Although this work certainly draws on the methodology of Sykes, Jacobs, DiIulio, and Lin, in which one studies the prison through immersion,[11] it also draws on the work of other criminal justice scholars who went beyond this to look at the interplay between the local community and criminal justice institutions.[12] This broader lens should not just extend to local communities, but to the political system as a whole.

Perhaps more importantly, we have lost sight of the fact that the police, courts, and prisons are, at least on the surface, all part of the same system. Although there has been some interest in the interaction between the court system and the police, prisons are usually left out of the discussion. Prisons are a vital part of this sometimes dysfunctional system of dealing with crime, and more interinstitutional studies just of the criminal justice system could shed more light on how these institutions work, or often do not work, together.

Prison studies need to go beyond recidivism rates and inmate population numbers. The literature on the prison-industrial complex does some of this, but prisons are still treated as an amorphous entity, as if all prisons are essentially the same. It may well be that political science and the "New Institutionalist" movement is the perfect place for these types of studies. One of the strengths of our discipline is in understanding how institutions interact, but we must first place prisons in their proper context—as a legal and political institution.

From the community's side, this dissertation has implications for other economic-development plans and the ensuing irony that the plans inevitably change the character of the town itself. These communities need outside entities to bring jobs and economic security, but they also bring new people into these small, often parochial towns. Additionally there may be other ancillary problems that are not discussed during the planning stages. In other words, the effect that an institution has on a community goes beyond just the number of jobs that it brings or the impact it has on the local economy.

This paradox is at play even when the institution being brought in is not governmental in nature. It may be that military bases or state hospitals will have similar issues to those that are discussed in this dissertation, but this may also be true with colleges and universities or other new "saviors" of the local economic-development scene, such as casinos. Small towns have become more active and creative in getting involved in the world of economic development. They no longer sit back and hope that a Microsoft-like corporation will open a large office in their town. But this activity and creativity may lead to some of the same issues that Florence and Beeville confront regularly, and the relationships that develop between the town and its supposed economic savior may go through a similar development that we have seen here.

In some ways, what we have seen in these two communities is what one interviewee called "state-sponsored welfare for rural communities."[13] Market factors have left these communities behind in a world of globalization where at the very least, access to transportation centers or a well-educated populace is a needed base on which to build an economy. There are good reasons those corporations, as Benny Johnson, mayor of Cañon City, so eloquently put it, "ain't exactly knocking at the door" and are unlikely to do so anytime soon. Of course, this begs the question: If these areas cannot compete for corporate dollars, why should the state essentially subsidize their continued existence? Or perhaps more to the point: If there are good reasons why corporations do not want to locate in these areas, why would the state and federal government want to?

The "knee-jerk" answer to these questions is that the incentive packages that have been put together to woo prisons to these rural communities are too good for the government to pass up, but this answer is too simplistic and takes us only so far. Rural communities often give corporations tax abatements and other incentives to move various outfits to their area, but with little success.[14] I question whether, over the long haul, the ancillary costs of locating prisons in rural areas will overcome the savings realized through these incentive packages and the pool of cheap labor. The federal government does not seem to take advantage of this labor pool from the start, and Texas has seen that there is a point at which the town runs out of qualified individuals to supply. I have seen no studies on the matter, but logic dictates that the transportation costs involved in moving inmates to and from these rural areas would grow over time to the point where the cheap land and utilities no longer pay off.

Even if the costs remain below what they might be in a more urban setting, there are still issues that need to be considered. In her new book *The Golden Gulag*, Ruth Gilmore discusses the devastating effects these rural prisons have on the inmates' relationship with their families.[15] We must remember that most of the inmates in these prisons will eventually get out. Unfortunately, statistically speaking, most will soon return. This cycle has led to prison slang such as "doing life on the installment plan," in which inmates do brief stints in the outside world sandwiched between long stints in prison. The utter disconnect that occurs between inmates and their families may be a factor in this, and having to take a bus many hours to visit a loved one does not much help. An inmate from Houston in far eastern Texas might end up in El Paso, some 10 hours away by car. This trip is simple compared to getting to Florence from any city outside of Colorado, which would include a plane flight and a three-hour drive from Denver, hardly something many families would be willing or able to do. There are also other issues mentioned at various points throughout this dissertation that seem not to hit many of the principal's awareness. Two stand out most profoundly. The first problem is that of having rural kids, in many cases, guarding much more sophisticated urban inmates. The second has to do with the ancillary damage being done to a substantial portion of the population in these rural communities when they work as COs.

Unfortunately, these problems may just be the "nature of the beast" with our burgeoning prison population and our current treatment of inmates. Those issues are significant and well beyond the reach of this study, but they may be more difficult when prisons are sited for economic reasons. This is a short-term solution to a long-term problem—the proverbial "band-aid on a broken arm" that the prison-building boom has caused. And that break is just one of the collateral effects of our current criminal justice system that seem to be just percolating below the surface. They will not just go away without major overhauls of the system and forward-thinking policy decisions.

NOTES

1. Williams, "Send Us Your Poor Huddled Detainees."
2. *Schwarzenegger v. Plata* (09–1233) (jurisdiction postponed).
3. A quick assessment of the zip codes of current employees would seem to be a good start to answer the second part of this, something that the TDCJ has done in Beeville. I do not know whether or not they share this information with potential prison towns.

4. In other words, I am willing to allow for the possibility that on a state level, other states, prison departments may not feel that their job includes fostering good community relations.

5. Interestingly, Warden Rios had just taken over FCI Florence when I was doing research there. He was the model of a citizen warden. He spent extensive time talking to me, he gave a group of my students a personal tour, and he came to speak to them in class.

6. Williams, "Citizen Wardens and Hermit Wardens: Which is Running Your Facility?"

7. Camp and Gaes, "Growth and Quality of U.S. Private Prisons: Evidence from a National Survey."

8. This is not to say that the federal government is not burdened by prisoner lawsuits. Congress passed the Prison Litigation Reform Act (PLRA) in 1996 to try to streamline the process because of complaints from the federal judiciary. For a detailed and empirical account, see Schlanger, "Inmate Litigation."

9. Hooks et al., "The Prison Industry: Carceral Expansion and Employment in U.S. Counties, 1969–1994."

10. Goffman, *Asylums*.

11. Sykes, *The Society of Captives: A Study of a Maximum Security Prison*. Jacobs, *Statesville: The Penitentiary in Mass Society*. DiIulio, *Governing Prisons: A Case Study of Correctional Management*. Lin, *Reform in the Making: The Implementation of Social Policy in Prison*.

12. Wilson, *The Variety of Police Behavior: The Management of Law and Order in Eight Communities*. Klonoski et al., *The Politics of Local Justice*. Lyons, *The Politics of Community Policing: Rearranging the Power to Punish*. Skogan, *Police and Community in Chicago: A Tale of Three Cities*.

13. Personal communication, DH, March 2004.

14. Of course, these communities cannot compete with overseas locations for certain types of jobs, and one would hope that states do not begin to locate prisons overseas to take advantage of the pool of cheap labor.

15. Gilmore, *Golden Gulag*.

References

Abrams, Kathleen Shea, and William Lyons. *Impact of Correctional Facilities on Land Values and Public Safety* North Miami, FL: FAU-FIU Joint Center for Environmental and Urban Problems, Florida International University, 1987.

American Correctional Association. *Directory: Juvenile and Adult Correctional Departments, Institutions, Agencies, and Paroling Authorities.* Lanham, MD: American Correctional Association, 1995.

American Friends Service Committee. *Struggle for Justice.* New York: Hill and Wang, 1971.

Austin, James, and John Irwin. *It's About Time: America's Imprisonment Binge.* New York: Wadsworth, 2000.

Avidon, Jacob E. *Economic and Social Impacts of Prisons on Small Cities.* New Brunswick, NJ: Center for Urban Policy Research, Rutgers, The State University of New Jersey, 1998.

Baird-Olson, K. *Doing What We Have Always Done: A Case Study of Rural Policing.* Washington, D.C.: U.S. Department of Justice, 2000

Banakar, R., and Max Travers, eds. *Theory and Method in Socio-Legal Research.* Oxford, United Kingdom: Hart, 2005.

Bartollas, Clemens, Stuart J. Miller, and Paul B. Wice. *Participants in American Criminal Justice: The Promise and the Performance.* Englewood Cliffs, NJ: Prentice Hall, 1983.

Baumgartner, Frank R., and Bryan D. Jones., eds. *Policy Dynamics.* Chicago: University of Chicago Press, 2002.

Beale, C. "Prisons, Population, and Jobs in Nonmetro America." *Rural Development Perspectives* 8 (1993): 16–19.

Beale, C. "Rural Prisons: An Update." *Rural Development Perspectives* 11 (1996): 25–27.

Beck, A., and P. Harrison. *Bureau of Justice Statistics Bulletin: Prisoners in 2000*. Washington, D.C.: U.S. Department of Justice, 2001.

Beck, Allen J., and Christopher J. Mumola. *Prisoners in 1998*. Bulletin, NCJ 175687, Washington, D.C.: U.S. Department of Justice, Bureau of Justice Statistics, 1999.

Beck, Melinda. "Kicking the Prison Habit." *Newsweek*, June 14, 1993, 32–37.

Belk, A. *Making it Plain: Deconstructing the Politics of the American Prison-Industrial Complex*. Dissertation. College Park: University of Maryland, 2003.

Besser, Terri, and M. Hanson. "The Development of Last Resort: The Impact of New State Prisons on Small Town Economies." Paper presented at the annual meeting of the Rural Sociological Society, Montreal, Canada, 2003.

Bloom, Barbara. "Community Managed Corrections: Empowering Approach to Community-Managed Corrections." *Humboldt Journal of Social Relations*, 17, no. 1 and 2 (1991): 263–277.

Blumstein, Alfred. "Prisons." *Crime*, edited by James Q. Wilson and Joan Petersilia. San Francisco: ICS Press, 1995.

Boester, Michael. *The Perceived Social Impact of Adult Male Correctional Centers on Three Southern Illinois' Communities*. MA Thesis, Edwardsville: Southern Illinois University, 2000.

Bohannan, Paul. *Justice and Judgment among the Tiv*. London: Oxford University Press, 1957.

Bowker, Lee H. *Prison Victimization*. New York: Elsevier, 1980.

Bright, C. *The Powers that Punish: Prison and Politics in the Era of the "Big House," 1920–1955*. Ann Arbor: University of Michigan Press, 1996.

Burke, Victoria Kairumba. *The Impact of State Prisons on the Economy of Kentucky*. Lexington: University of Kentucky, 2001.

Carlson, K. "What Happens and What Counts: Resident Assessments of Prison Impacts on Their Communities." *Humboldt Journal of Social Relations* 17 (1991): 115–144.

Carlson, K. "Doing Good and Looking Bad: A Case Study of Prison/Community Relations." *Crime & Delinquency* 38 (1992): 56–69.

Carlson, K. "Prisons and Rural Communities: Making the Most and Losing the Least from a Growth Industry," in *Rural Development Strategies*, edited by J. N. Reid and D. W. Sears, 189–203. Chicago: Nelson-Hall Publishers, 1995.

Camp, S. D., and G. G. Gaes. "Growth and Quality of U.S. Private Prisons: Evidence from a National Survey." *Criminology & Public Policy* 1 (2002): 427–449.

Campbell, Rosemae. *From Trappers to Tourists: Fremont County, 1830–1950*. Cañon City, CO: Fremont/Custer Historical Society, 1998.

Chuang, Su Chong. "The Distribution of Texas State Prisons: Economic Impact Analysis of State Prison Sitting on Local Communities." PhD dissertation, Arlington: University of Texas–Arlington, 1998.

Clark, Olivia. "Salem and State Prisons: A Test Case for Community Relations." *Humboldt Journal of Social Relations*, 17, no. 1 and 2 (1991), 197–210.

Clear, Todd R., and George F. Cole. *American Corrections*, 4th ed. Belmont, CA: Wadsworth Publishing Company, 1997.

Clemmer, D. *The Prison Community.* New York: Holt, Rinehart, and Winston, 1958.

Collier, D., H. E. Brady, and J. Seawright, eds. *Rethinking Social Inquiry: Diverse Tools, Shared Standards.* Lanham, MD: Rowman & Littlefield, Berkeley Public Policy, 2004.

Conley, John, and William O'Barr. *Rules versus Relationships: The Ethnography of Legal Discourse.* Chicago: University of Chicago Press, 1990.

Conley, John, and William O'Barr. "Legal Anthropology Comes Home: A Brief History of the Ethnographic Study of Law." *Loyola of Los Angeles Law Review* 27, no. 41 (1993).

Conover, Ted. *Newjack: Guarding Sing Sing.* New York: Random House, 2000.

Cronin, Thomas E., Tania Z. Cronin, and Michael E. Milakovich. *U.S. v. Crime in the Streets.* Bloomington: Indiana University Press, 1981.

Dahl, Robert. *Who Governs? Democracy and Power in an American City.* New Haven, CT: Harper and Row, 1961.

Daniel, William. "Prisons and Crime Rates in Rural Areas: The Case of Lassen County." *Humboldt Journal of Social Relations* 17, no. 1 and 2 (1991): 129–170.

DiIulio, John. *Governing Prisons: A Case Study of Correctional Management.* New York: The Free Press, 1987.

DiIulio, John. *No Escape: The Future of American Corrections.* New York: Basic Books, 1991.

DiIulio, John. "Crime and Punishment in Wisconsin." *Wisconsin Policy Research Report* 3 (December 1990).

Dolbeare, K. *Trial Courts in Urban Politics.* New York: John Wiley and Sons, 1967.

Doyle, Z. "Does Crime Pay: Pros and Cons of Rural Prisons." *Economic Development Digest* 8 (2002): 1–4.

Dyer, J. *The Perpetual Prisoner Machine: How America Profits from Crime.* Boulder, CO: Westview Press, 2001.

Edgerton, K. *Montana Justice: Power, Punishment, and the Penitentiary.* Seattle: University of Washington Press, 2004.

Eisinger, Peter. *The Rise of the Entrepreneurial State: State and Local Economic Development Policy in the United States.* Madison: University of Wisconsin Press, 1988.

Elkin, S. *City and Regime in the American Republic.* Chicago, IL: University of Chicago Press, 1987.

Ewald, A. "Civil Death: The Ideological Paradox of Criminal Disenfranchisement Law in the United States," *Wisconsin Law Review* 1045 (2002): 1045–1137.

Falcone, D., E. Wells, and R. Weisheit. "The Small-Town Police Department." *Policing: An International Journal of Police Strategies and Management* 25 (2002): 371–384.

Farmer, David John. *The Language of Public Administration: Bureaucracy, Modernity, and Postmodernity.* Tuscaloosa: University of Alabama Press, 1995.

Farrington, K. "The Modern Prison as Total Institution? Public Perception versus Objective Reality." *Crime & Delinquency* 38, no. 1 (1992): 6–26.

Feeley, M., and E. L. Rubin. *Judicial Policy-Making and the Modern State: How the Courts Reformed America's Prisons.* Cambridge, United Kingdom: Cambridge University Press, 1998.

Feicock, Richard. "The Effects of Economic Development Policy of Local Economic Growth." *American Journal of Political Science* 35, no. 3 (1991): 645–655.

Fenno, R. *Home Style: House Members in Their Districts.* New York: Little, Brown, 1978.

Flanagan, Timothy J. *Long-Term Imprisonment: Policy, Science, and Correctional Practice.* Thousand Oaks, CA: Sage Publications, 1995.

Flanagan, Timothy J. "Reform or Punish: Americans' Views of the Correctional System," in *Americans View Crime and Justice: A National Public Opinion Survey,* edited by Timothy J. Flanagan and Dennis R. Longmire. Thousand Oaks, CA: Sage Publications, 1996.

Fleischer, M. *Warehousing Violence.* Newbury Park, CA: Sage Publications, 1989.

Foucault, Michel. *Discipline & Punish: The Birth of the Prison*, translated by Alan Sheridan. New York: Pantheon, 1977.

Fraser, Joelle. "An American Seduction: Portrait of a Prison Town," in *Prison Nation*, edited by Tara Herivel and Paul Wright, 73–84. New York: Routledge, 2003.

Garland, David. *Punishment and Modern Society.* Chicago: University of Chicago Press, 1990.

Garland, David. *The Culture of Control: Crime and Social Order in Contemporary Society.* Chicago: University of Chicago Press, 2001.

Geertz, C. *Local Knowledge: Further Essays in Interpretive Anthropology.* New York: Basic Books, 2000.

Gibbons, Stephen, and Gregory Pierce. "Politics and Prison Development in a Rural Area." *The Prison Journal* 75, no. 3 (1995): 300–389.

Gilmore, R. W. *Golden Gulag.* Berkeley: University of California Press, 2007.

Gluckman, M. *The Judicial Process among the Barotse of Northern Rhodesia.* Manchester, United Kingdom: University Press for the Rhodes Livingston Institute, 1955.

Gluckman, M. *The Ideas in Barotse Jurisprudence.* New Haven, CT: Yale University Press, 1965.

Goffman, Erving. *Asylums.* New York: Anchor, 1961.

Greenhouse, C. *Praying for Justice.* Ithaca, NY: Cornell University Press, 1986.

Greenhouse, Carol J., Barbara Yngvesson, and David M. Engel. *Law and Community in Three American Towns.* Ithaca, NY: Cornell University Press, 1994.

Guerra, Carlos." State Has Helped Beeville Develop a 'Working-Poor' Economy." *San Antonio Express-News,* January 6, 2002, 1B.

Hammett, Theodore M., Rebecca Widom, Joel Epstein, Michael Gross, Santiago Sifre, and Tammy Enos. *1994 Update: HIV/AIDS and STD's in Correctional Facilities.* NCJ 156832. Washington, D.C.: U.S. Department of Justice, National Institute of Justice, and U.S. Department of Health and Human Services, Centers for Disease Control and Prevention, 1995.

Harris, Thomas R., and Shawn W. Stoddard. *Estimation of Economic Impacts of a Federal Prison in Churchill County.* Reno: University of Nevada–Reno, University Center for Economic Development, 1993.

Harrison, Deborah. *The First Casualty: Violence against Women in Canadian Military Communities.* Toronto: James Lorimer & Co., 2002.

Heumann, M. *Plea Bargaining: The Experiences of Prosecutors, Judges and Defense Attorneys.* Chicago: University of Chicago Press, 1978.

Heumann, Milton, Brian Pinaire, and Tom S. Clark. "Beyond the Sentence," *Criminal Law Bulletin* 41, no. 1 (2005): 24–46.

Holyoke, Thomas T. "Choosing Battlegrounds: Interest Group Lobbying across Multiple Venues." *Political Research Quarterly* 56 (2003): 325–336.

Hooks, Greg, Clayton Mosher, Thomas Rotolo, and Linda Labao. "The Prison Industry: Carceral Expansion and Employment in U.S. Counties, 1969–1994." *Social Science Quarterly* 85 (2004): 37–57.

Huling, T. L. *Prisons as a Growth Industry in Rural America: An Exploratory Discussion of the Effects on Young African American Men in Inner Cities.* Washington, D.C.: U.S. Commission on Civil Rights, 1999.

Huling, T. L. "Building a Prison Economy in Rural America." *Invisible Punishment: The Collateral Consequences of Mass Imprisonment,* edited by Marc Mauer and Meda Chesney-Lind. New York: The New Press, 2002.

Hunter, Floyd. *Community Power Structure.* Chapel Hill: University of North Carolina Press, 1953.

Jacobs, James. "The Politics of Corrections Town Prison Relations as a Determinant of Reform." *Social Service Review* 15 (1976): 623–631.

Jacobs, James. *Statesville: The Penitentiary in Mass Society.* Chicago: University of Chicago Press, 1977.

Jacobs, James. *New Perspectives on Prisons and Imprisonment.* Ithaca, NY: Cornell University Press, 1983.

Jacobson, M. *Downsizing Prisons: How to Reduce Crime and End Mass Incarceration.* New York: New York University Press, 2005.

Johnson, Thomas G., and James Scott. "The Changing Nature of Rural Communities." *Increasing Understanding of Public Problems and Policies* (1997): 177–188.

Josi, Don A., and Dale K. Sechrest. *The Changing Career of the Correctional Officer: Policy Implications for the 21st Century.* Boston: Butterworth-Heinemann, 1998.

Kauffman, Kelsey. *Prison Officers and Their World.* Cambridge, MA: Harvard University Press, 1988.

Kelling, George L. "Police Field Services and Crime: The Presumed Effects of a Capacity." *Crime & Delinquency* 24, no. 2 (1978): 173–184.

King, Gary, Robert O. Keohane, and Sidney Verba. *Designing Social Inquiry: Scientific Inference in Qualitative Research.* Princeton, NJ: Princeton University Press, 1994.

King, Ryan, Marc Mauer, and Tracy Huling. *Big Prisons, Small Towns: Prison Economics in Rural America.* Washington, D.C.: The Sentencing Project, 2003.

Klonoski, James R., and Robert I. Mendelsohn, eds. *The Politics of Local Justice.* Boston: Little, Brown and Co., 1970.

Krause, Jerrald. "Community Opposition to Correctional Facility Siting: Beyond the NIMBY Syndrome." *Humboldt Journal of Social Relations* 17, no. 1 and 2 (1991): 239–262.

Krause, Jerrald. "The Effects of Prison Siting Practices on Community Status Arrangements: A Framework Applied to the Siting of California State Prisons." *Crime & Delinquency* 38, no. 1 (1992): 27–55.

Lansing, Doug, Joseph B. Bogan, and Loren Karacki. "Unit Management: Implementing a Different Correctional Approach." *Federal Probation* 41 (1977): 43–49.

Lawrence, S., and J. Travis. *The New Landscape of Imprisonment: Mapping America's Prison Expansion.* Washington, D.C.: The Urban Institute, 2004. Available at http://www.urban.org/UploadedPDF/410994_mapping_prisons.pdf.

Lilly, J. Robert, and Paul Knepper. "The Corrections-Commercial Complex." *Crime & Delinquency* 39, no. 2 (1993): 158–166.

Lin, A. C. *Reform in the Making: The Implementation of Social Policy in Prison.* Princeton, NJ: Princeton University Press, 2000.

Lindblom, Charles. "The Market as Prison." *Journal of Politics* 44 (1982): 324–336.

Lipton, Douglas, Robert Martinson, and Judith Wilks. *The Effectiveness of Correctional Treatment.* New York: Praeger, 1975.

Llewellyn, Karl, and E. Adamson Hoebel. *The Cheyenne Way: Conflict and Case Law in Primitive Jurisprudence.* Norman: University of Oklahoma Press, 1941.

Lofting, Everard M., and Loren L. Parks. *The Economic and Fiscal Impacts of a State Prison in Del Norte County.* Berkeley, CA: The Associates, 1986.

Lyons, William. *The Politics of Community Policing: Rearranging the Power to Punish.* Ann Arbor: University of Michigan Press, 1999.

Maguire, Kathleen, and Ann L. Pastore, eds. *Sourcebook of Criminal Justice Statistics, 1994.* NCJ 154591. Washington, D.C.: U.S. Department of Justice, Bureau of Justice Statistics, 1995.

Maguire, Kathleen, and Ann L. Pastore, eds. *Sourcebook of Criminal Justice Statistics 1995*. NCJ 158900. Washington, D.C.: U.S. Department of Justice, Bureau of Justice Statistics, 1996.

Maine, Sir Henry. *Ancient Law*. New York: Dutton, 1861.

Manna, Paul. *School's In: Federalism and the National Education Agenda*. Washington, D.C.: Georgetown University Press, 2006.

Martinson, Robert. "What Works? Questions and Answers about Prison Reform. *Public Interest* 35 (1974): 22–54.

Martinson, Robert. "California Research at the Crossroads." *Crime & Delinquency* 22 (1976): 180–191.

Mauer, Marc, and Meda Chesney-Lind, eds. *Invisible Punishment: The Collateral Consequences of Mass Imprisonment*. New York: The New Press, 2002.

Maxim, Paul. "Prisons and Their Perceived Impact on Local Community: A Case Study." *Social Indicators Research* 13 (1983): 39–58.

McCarthy, Belinda, and Robert Langworthy. *Older Offenders*. New York: Praeger, 1988.

McCleery, Richard H. "The Governmental Process and Informal Social Control," in *The Prison: Studies in Institution Organization and Change*, edited by Donald R. Cressey. New York: Holt, Rinehart and Winston, 1961.

McGee, Richard. *Prisons and Politics*. Lexington MA: Heath and Company, 1981.

McShane, M., and F. Williams. "Prison Impact Studies: Some Comments on Methodological Rigor." *Crime & Delinquency* 38, no. 1 (1992): 105–121.

Merry, S. *Getting Justice and Getting Even: Legal Consciousness among Working-Class Americans*. Chicago: University of Chicago Press, 1990.

Millay, John. "From Asylum to Penitentiary: The Social Impact of Eastern Oregon Correctional Institutions upon Pendleton." *Humboldt Journal of Social Relations* 17, no. 1 and 2 (1989): 171–196.

Miller, Gary J. *Managerial Dilemmas*. Cambridge, United Kingdom: Cambridge University Press, 1992.

Miller, Lisa L. *The Politics of Community Crime Prevention: Implementing Weed and Seed in Seattle*. Burlington, VT: Dartmouth/Ashgate Press Law Justice and Power Series, 2001.

Miller, Lisa L. *The Perils of Federalism*. New York: Oxford University Press, 2007.

Mitford, Jessica. *Kind and Usual Punishment: The Prison Business*. New York: Alfred A. Knopf, 1973.

Moore, Sally Falk. "Certainties Undone: Fifty Turbulent Years of Legal Anthropology, 1949–1999." *Journal of the Royal Anthropology Institute* 7 (2001): 95–117.

Morris, Norval. *The Future of Imprisonment*. Chicago: University of Chicago Press, 1974.

Moser, Margaret. *The Biography of a Particular Place: Bee County from the Days of the Spanish Missions through September 11, 2001*. Beeville, TX: Bee Publishing Co., 2001.

Nader, Laura. "Controlling Processes in the Practice of Law: Hierarchy and Pacification in the Movement to Re-Form Dispute Ideology." *The Ohio State Journal on Dispute Resolution* 9 (1993): 1–25.

O'Hare, Michael, Lawrence Bacow, and Debra Sanderson. *Facilities Siting and Public Opposition.* New York: Van Nostrand Reinhold Company, 1983.

O'Shea, T. "Community Policing in Small Town Rural America." *Policing and Society* 9 (1999): 59–76.

Ostrum, E. "Converting Threats into Opportunities." *PS: Political Science & Politics* 39, no. 1 (2006): 3–12. APSA 2005 James Madison Award lecture.

Parks, Loren L. *The Economic Impacts of State Prisons in Kings County, California.* Carmichael, CA: Analytics Economic Analysis, 1990.

Parks, R. B., S. D. Mastrofski, C. DeJong, and M. K. Gray. "How Officers Spend Their Time with the Community." *Justice Quarterly* 16 (1999): 483–518.

Payne, Brian K., Bruce L. Berg, and Ivan Y. Sun. "Policing in Small Town America: Dogs, Drunks, Disorder, and Dysfunction." *Journal of Criminal Justice* 33, no. 1 (2005): 31–41.

Peters, Tom. *Liberation Management: Necessary Disorganization for the Nanosecond Nineties.* New York: Alfred A. Knopf, 1992.

Peters, Tom. *Thriving on Chaos: Handbook for a Management Revolution.* New York: Harper & Row, 1997.

Pinaire, Brian, Milton Heumann, and Laura Bilotta. "Barred from the Vote: Public Attitudes toward the Disenfranchisement of Felons." *Fordham Urban Law Journal* 30 (2003): 1519–1550.

Pralle, Sarah. *Branching Out and Digging In: Environmental Advocacy and Agenda Setting.* Washington, D.C.: Georgetown University Press, 2006.

Rasmussen, Thomas. "Not In My Backyard: The Politics of Siting Prisons, Landfills and Incinerators." *State and Local Government Review* 24, no. 3 (1992): 128–134.

Redding, Nick. *Methland: Death and Life of an American Small Town.* New York: Bloomsbury USA, 2010.

Rephann, T., J. Dalton, A. Stair, and A. Isserman. "Casino Gambling as an Economic Development Strategy." *Tourism Economics* 3 (1997): 161–183.

Ringquist, Evan. "Political Control and Policy Impact in EPA's Office of Water Quality." *American Journal of Political Science* 39, no. 2 (1995): 336–363.

Riveland, Chase. "Prison Management Trends, 1975–2025." *Crime & Justice,* 26 (1999): 163–203.

Roberts, John W. *Reform and Retribution: An Illustrated History of American Prisons.* Lanham, MD: American Correctional Association, 1997.

Rogers, George, and Marshall Haimes. "Local Impact of a Low Security Federal Correctional Institution." *Federal Probation* 51, no. 3 (1987): 28–34.

Schlanger, M. "Inmate Litigation." *Harvard Law Review* 116, no. 6 (2003): 1555–1706.

Scholz, John T., and B. Dan Wood. "Efficiency, Equity, and Politics: Democratic Controls over the Tax Collector." *American Journal of Political Science* 43, no. 4 (1999): 1166–1188.

Sechrest, Dale. "Understanding the Corrections and Community Response to Prison Siting." *Humboldt Journal of Social Relations* 17, no. 1 and 2 (1991): 1–16.

Sechrest, Dale. "Locating Prisons: Open versus Closed Approaches to Siting." *Crime & Delinquency* 38, no. 1 (1992): 88–104.

Seidel, Karen M., and Ronald L. Chastain. *Local Economic and Fiscal Impacts of a Minimum-Security Correctional Facility in Region One.* Eugene, OR: Bureau of Governmental Research and Service, University of Oregon, 1988.

Setti, C. "Prisons and Their Effects on Local Economics: The Colorado Experience." *CPEC Center for Tax Policy Research of Denver* 47, no. 3 (2001): 271–291.

Shicor, David. "Myths and Realities in Prison Siting." *Crime & Delinquency* 38, no. 1 (1992): 70–87.

Simon, Leonore M. J. "Prison Behavior and the Victim-Offender Relationship among Violent Offenders." *Justice Quarterly* 10 (1993): 489–506.

Simon, Jonathan. "The 'Society of Captives' in the Era of Hyper-Incarceration." *Theoretical Criminology* 4, no. 3 (2000): 285–308.

Skogan, W. *Police and Community in Chicago: A Tale of Three Cities.* New York: Oxford University Press, 2006.

Skogan, Wesley, and Susan Hartnett. *Community Policing: Chicago Style.* New York: Oxford University Press, 1997.

Skogan, W., and K. Frydell, eds. *Fairness and Effectiveness in Policing: The Evidence.* Washington, D.C.: The National Academies Press, 2004

Smyka, John Ortiz, David Cheng, Carl Ferguson Jr., Carolyn Trent, Barbara French, and Annette Waters. "The Effects of a Prison Facility on the Regional Economy." *Journal of Criminal Justice* 12, no. 6 (1984): 521–540.

State Board of Equalization. *Prison Impact Study.* Sacramento, CA: Board of Equalization, 2002. Available at http://www.boe.ca.gov/pdf/prisonimpactstudy.pdf.

Stephen, James J. *State Prison Expenditures, 1996.* NCJ 172211. Washington, D.C.: U.S. Department of Justice, Bureau of Justice Statistics, 1999.

Stone, Clarence. "Systemic Power and Community Decision Making: A Restatement of Stratification Theory." *American Political Science Review* 78, no. 4 (1980): 978–990.

Stone, Clarence. "Preemptive Power: Floyd Hunter's Community Power Structure Reconsidered." *American Journal of Political Science* 32 (1988): 82–104.

Swanson, Cheryl. "Citizens Perceptions of Prison Effects on Their Community." *State and Local Government Review* 25, no. 2 (1993): 107–116.

Sykes, G. *The Society of Captives: A Study of a Maximum Security Prison.* Princeton, NJ: Princeton University Press, 1958.

Thies, J. S. *The Big House in a Small Town: The Economic and Social Impacts of a Correctional Facility on its Host Community.* PhD dissertation. University of Missouri–Saint Louis, 1998.

Thies, J. S. "Prisons and Host Communities: Debunking the Myths and Building Community Relations." *Corrections Today* 62 (2000): 136–139.

Tonry, Michael. "Twenty Years of Sentencing Reform: Steps Forward, Steps Backward." *Judicature* 78 (1995): 169–172.

U.S. Census Department. *Census of Population and Housing, Small Area Income and Poverty Estimates.* Washington, D.C.: U.S. Census Department, 1990. Available at http://www.census.gov.

U.S. Census Department. *Census of Population and Housing, Small Area Income and Poverty Estimates.* Washington, D.C.: U.S. Census Department, 2000. Available at http://www.census.gov.

U.S. Department of Justice, Bureau of Justice Statistics. *Census of State and Federal Adult Correctional Facilities, 1995.* ICPSR 6953. Ann Arbor, MI: Interuniversity Consortium for Political and Social Research. Washington, D.C.: U.S. Department of Justice, 1998.

Useem, Bert, and Peter Kimball. *States of Siege: U.S. Prison Riots, 1971–1986.* New York: Oxford University Press, 1989.

Van den Haag, Ernest. *Punishing Criminals: Concerning a Very Old and Painful Question.* New York: Basic Books, 1975.

Varenne, Hervé. *Americans Together: Structured Diversity in a Midwestern Town.* New York: Teachers College Press, 1977.

Von Hirsch, Andrew. *Doing Justice: The Choice of Punishments.* New York: Hill and Wang, 1976.

Wagner, Peter. *Detaining for Dollars: Federal Aid Follows Inner-City Prisoners to Rural Town Coffers.* Springfield, MA: Prison Policy Initiative, 2002.

Wagner, Peter. *Importing Constituents: Prisoners and Political Clout in New York.* Springfield, MA: Prison Policy Initiative, 2002.

Walzer, Norman, ed. *Rural Community Economic Development.* New York: Praeger Publishers, 1991.

Weisheit, R. *Studying Drugs in Rural Areas: Notes from the Field.* Washington, D.C.: U.S. Government Printing Office, 1997.

Weisheit, R., D. Falcone, and L. Wells. *Crime and Policing in Rural and Small Town America.* Prospect Heights, IL: Waveland, 1996.

Weisheit, R., L. Wells, and D. Falcone. "Community Policing in Small Town and Rural America." *Crime & Delinquency* 40 (1994): 549–567.

Weisheit, R., L. Wells, and D. Falcone. *Crime and Policing in Rural and Small Town America.* Washington, D.C.: National Institute of Justice, 1995.

Whitaker, G. P. "What is Patrol Work?" *Police Studies* 4 (1982): 13–22.

Whitford, A. "Competing Explanations for Bureaucratic Preferences." *Journal of Theoretical Politics* 19, no. 3 (2007): 219–247.

Wildprett, Bill, and John LaRocque. *Coyote Ridge Corrections Center 1991–93 Fiscal Impacts Analysis.* Olympia, WA: Research and Evaluation, Washington State Department of Community Development, 1992.

Williams, Eric. "Send Us Your Poor Huddled Detainees." *Los Angeles Times,* June 29, 2009, A26.

Williams, Eric. "Citizen Wardens and Hermit Wardens: Which Is Running Your Facility?" Available at http://www.correctionsone.com/facility-design-and-operation/articles/2067809-Citizen-wardens-and-hermit-wardens-Which-is-running-your-facility/.

Wilson, James Q. *The Variety of Police Behavior: The Management of Law and Order in Eight Communities.* Cambridge, MA: Harvard University Press, 1968.

Wilson, James Q. *Thinking about Crime.* New York: Basic Books, 1975.

Wilson, James Q., and George L. Kelling. "Broken Windows." *Atlantic Monthly* 249, no. 3 (1982): 29–38.

Wood, B. Dan, and Richard W. Waterman. *Bureaucratic Dynamics: The Role of Bureaucracy in a Democracy.* Boulder, CO: Westview Press, 1994.

Wright, Kevin N. *Effective Prison Leadership.* New York: William Neil Publishing, 1994.

Wright, Kevin N. "The World of Work Has Changed! So What Does This Mean for Correctional Management?" *Correctional Management Quarterly* 1 (1997): 32–39.

Yanarella, Ernest J., and Susan Blankenship. "Big House on the Rural Landscape: Prison Recruitment as a Policy Tool of Local Economic Development." *Journal of Appalachian Studies* 12, no. 2 (2005): 110–139.

Index

About the Author

ERIC J. WILLIAMS is an assistant professor in the Department of Criminology and Criminal Justice Studies at Sonoma State University in Rohnert Park, California. His work has appeared in the *Los Angeles Times* and numerous other papers nationwide.